READING AMY TAN

Recent Titles in
The Pop Lit Book Club

Reading Barbara Kingsolver
Lynn Marie Houston and Jennifer Warren

READING AMY TAN

Lan Dong

The Pop Lit Book Club

GREENWOOD PRESS
An Imprint of ABC-CLIO, LLC

A B C 🔖 C L I O

Santa Barbara, California • Denver, Colorado • Oxford, England

Library of Congress Cataloging-in-Publication Data

Dong, Lan.
  Reading Amy Tan / Lan Dong.
    p. cm. — (The Pop Lit Book Club)
  Includes bibliographical references and index.
ISBN 978-0-313-35546-2 (hard copy : alk. paper)—ISBN 978-0-313-35547-9
(ebook)
1. Tan, Amy—Criticism and interpretation. 2. Chinese American
women in literature. 3. Chinese Americans in literature. I. Title.
PS3570.A48Z656   2009
813'.54—dc22   2009010175

13 12 11 10 09   1 2 3 4 5

This book is also available on the World Wide Web as an eBook.
Visit www.abc-clio.com for details.

ABC-CLIO, LLC
130 Cremona Drive, P.O. Box 1911
Santa Barbara, California 93116–1911

This book is printed on acid-free paper ∞

Manufactured in the United States of America

CONTENTS

PREFACE

To say that Amy Tan is one of the most significant Asian American women writers would be an understatement. Her fame and success extend beyond ethnic and gender labels. Tan's influence on contemporary American literature and culture is far reaching. Her name appears repeatedly on college course reading lists. Some of her works have been incorporated into school curricula at various levels and have been embraced by book club members. Her writing also has been translated into many languages, which has expanded her readership worldwide. One of the unique aspects of Tan's writing is that her best-selling books often earn critical praise as well. To general readers, Tan is undoubtedly one of the most popular Asian American writers. Her debut book, *The Joy Luck Club* (1989), is one of the best known Chinese American texts. The fact that the National Endowment for the Arts (NEA) chose *The Joy Luck Club* for its 2007 Big Read program confirms the popularity and significance of this work. In academia, Tan's writing has been the topic of a large number of books, book chapters, journal articles, and master's and doctoral theses. A search of the *Modern Language Association International Bibliography* conducted on July 3, 2008, for example, generated 140 results on the subject of "Amy Tan," and 96 on "The Joy Luck Club." Not surprisingly, a variety of critical topics and theoretical perspectives regarding Tan's works have kindled engaging discussions among students, critics, and scholars in many academic disciplines as well as interdisciplinary fields.

Through its striking storytelling and unique characters, Amy Tan's fiction deals with such important themes as the complexity of human relationships, especially the connection and conflict between mothers and daughters and the bond between sisters; bicultural heritage, immigrants' experience, and interracial/interethnic relationships; ethnic exoticism and stereotypes, cultural authenticity, and assimilation; fate and faith; as well as friendship and female lineage. Tan is a versatile writer in terms of genres: she not only has published remarkable novels and short stories, but also is the author of a collection of essays and has produced a screenplay, an opera libretto, children's books, and television shows in collaboration with others. In particular, her renowned fiction, some of which is inspired by the life experiences of herself and her family, adds new meaning to the contemporary American novel and short story. Tan's earlier works, mostly casting Chinese and Chinese American characters, are rich in intriguing storytelling, explorations of the connection between past and present, and the characters' struggles over family relations and identity construction. Her novel *Saving Fish from Drowning* (2005) was a departure from her previous works in its portrayal of an American tourist group's adventure in Burma.

As part of The Pop Lit Book Club series, *Reading Amy Tan* aims to enrich high school curricula and book club activities by providing a comprehensive view of the writer and her works. Compared to other texts written on the author, *Reading Amy Tan* not only includes analysis and discussion of the writer's novels and other works, but it also provides up-to-date information regarding Tan's life and her writing while addressing her relation to popular culture, the media, the Internet, and today's issues. Also included are relevant resources found in literary studies, book reviews, interviews, media sources, and the World Wide Web for further reading. In addition, this book recommends books and movies based on the cultural and literary characteristics of Tan's writing.

This book is divided into several sections. Each part has a different focus on Tan and her writing, beginning with "A Writer's Life" that presents an overview of the author's life, influences, and writing career, and ends with discussion questions on how the author's life relates to her work. "Amy Tan and the Novel and Short Story" discusses the genres in which the author writes, in particular, the novel, short story, and prose. It also addresses the features of these genres, other related works in the genres, and how the author has followed and deviated from generic conventions. Discussion questions on the author's relation to literary forms help promote further thinking and research. The next five chapters on her novels offer plot summaries, discussions of characters, themes, and settings, as well as sidebars of interesting related material about the books, stories, and essays that Tan has published. Concluding each chapter are discussion questions about Tan's works, their cultural and social contexts, as well as their contributions to contemporary literature.

"Today's Issues in Amy Tan's Work" focuses on how the author's works reflect current events and issues, as well as the educational use of Tan's writing in the classroom. "Pop Culture in Amy Tan's Work" examines the film and stage adaptations of Tan's novel *The Joy Luck Club;* stage, opera, and television adaptations of her other works; and the role of popular culture in her writing. "Amy Tan on the Internet" discusses fan sites, official Web sites, and other Internet resources relevant to the author with discussion questions on the contents and usefulness of these sites. "Amy Tan and the Media" describes her book reviews, television appearances, and interviews, including discussion questions on how the author uses the media and how the media have treated the author. Based on characteristics of the author's writings, recommendations of other works are listed in "What Do I Read Next?" Last but not least, "Resources" provides a bibliography of print and electronic resources on Tan and her writing.

1

AMY TAN: A WRITER'S LIFE

Born on February 19, 1952, in Oakland, California, Amy Tan is the middle child of three; she is the only daughter of her parents who arrived in the United States from China only a few years before. Her brother Peter was born in 1950, and brother John Jr. was born in 1954. Her parents named her Amy Ruth Tan in English and An-mei (meaning "Blessing from America") in Chinese. Amy Tan first established her fame as a fiction writer by publishing *The Joy Luck Club* in 1989 with great success. She drew inspiration from the life experiences of her mother, herself, and many others that she knew. Her striking stories about mothers and daughters in *The Joy Luck Club* resonate with millions of readers, immigrants or otherwise. Reflecting on her family's influence on her writing career, Amy remarks: "In my family, there were two pillars of beliefs: Christian faith on my father's side, Chinese fate on my mother's" (Tan, *The Opposite of Fate*, 11).

Amy's father, John Yuehhan Tan, the oldest child of twelve, was born in Beijing in 1913. John's mother was a traditional Chinese healer. His father, Hugh Tan, not only converted to Christianity at a young age but also received English education in China and became a Presbyterian minister. Growing up with a strong influence of Christianity from his father, John eventually entered the ministry years later. First, having acquired English in childhood, John worked as a translator for the U.S. Information Service in China during World War II and immigrated to the United States in 1947 when he received a scholarship to study electrical engineering at the Massachusetts Institute of Technology. Shortly after arriving in San Francisco, John decided to give up the scholarship and study theology instead at the Berkeley Baptist Divinity School, later becoming a Baptist minister. Amy remembers her father being an easygoing and loving person. As a father, John worked hard to support his family and volunteered his time for the ministry. A devoted Christian, John's faith is "absolute," as Amy has described it. In John's definition, "Faith is the confident assurance that something we want is going to happen. It is the certainty that what we hope for is waiting for us even though we still cannot see it ahead of us" (*Fate*, 23). Growing up, Amy was quite fond of her father whose sermons influenced her storytelling in her fiction writing years later.

Amy's mother, Daisy Du Ching Tan (maiden name Li Bingzi), was born into a wealthy upper-class family in Shanghai in 1916. However, her childhood quickly turned into a tragic experience. Daisy's father died of influenza when she and her brother were young. Her mother Gu Jing-mei, a young and beautiful widow, had to raise her young children on her own. Jing-mei was forced to become a rich manufacturer's concubine after he raped her, thereafter becaming an outcast to her own family. Daisy spent a short time with her mother, living in the rich man's house. After Jing-mei gave birth to a son, the rich man's only male heir, one of his principal wives claimed the infant. When Jing-mei committed suicide by swallowing raw opium concealed in the New Year's rice cakes, Daisy was only nine years old. Jing-mei's last words to her young daughter, who wept at her deathbed, were: "Don't follow my footsteps" (*Fate*, 102). Watching her mother die inflicted an incurable trauma and a burden of shame on Daisy's life. Daisy's relatives raised her with sufficient material comforts, but she nonetheless grew up a lonely girl. She worked as a nurse in Shanghai for a short period of time before her marriage was arranged by her relatives. In 1935 when she was nineteen, Daisy was married to Wang Zo, a pilot for the Kuomintang air force, with whom she had five children before she left him because he was abusive. Two of these children died in infancy.

During the Sino-Japanese War (1937–1945), Daisy met John Tan. They fell in love at first sight around 1941 but endured a long time of separation before they ran into each other again on the street in Tianjin in northern China in 1945. Their brief love affair ended with Daisy's imprisonment upon a charge of adultery and John's voyage to the United States, brokenhearted. Released after serving two years in prison, Daisy finally made her escape from her disastrous marriage and joined John in the United States in 1949, having to leave behind her three surviving daughters. Daisy's tragic experiences directly inspired the stories of the characters An-mei Hsu and Suyuan Woo in *The Joy Luck Club* and Winnie Louie (Jiang Weili) in *The Kitchen God's Wife* (1991).

Daisy's belief in fate has had a strong influence on Amy's life as well as her writing: "In all of my writings, both fiction and nonfiction, directly or obliquely but always obsessively, I return to questions of fate and its alternatives" (*Fate,* 2). Daisy held a strong belief in spirits and ghosts, and insisted on moving whenever she was convinced that an evil spirit was haunting her house. Moreover, she was always persistent. Amy described her mother as a combative, petite woman who is "just determined as hell" (Somogyi and Stanton, 24). As a result, Amy's family moved frequently during her childhood among different places in California: Oakland, Fresno, Palo Alto, Santa Rosa, to name only a few, before they finally settled down in Santa Clara. By Amy's count, by the time she graduated from high school, she had attended eleven different schools (*Fate,* 22). Constantly being a new kid and having to adjust to a new school environment, Amy became a keen observer at a young age. This experience turned out to be beneficial for her career as a writer.

Daisy also had a profound influence on Amy's imagination, another key element for her writing career. As Amy said, her mother affected her imagination to such a degree that she could hear and see things that others would not; for example, coincidences, ironies in lies, and truths in contradictions (*Fate,* 33–34). Even now, after Daisy has passed away, Amy still feels she knows certain things; they are in her bones (*Fate,* 36). Daisy's significant influence on her daughter's life and writing career is best summarized by the author herself when she was writing her mother's obituary by her deathbed:

> In trying to write an obituary, I appreciated that there was still much I did not know about my mother. Though I had written books informed by her life, she remained a source of revelation and surprise. Of course I longed to know more about her, for her past had shaped me: her sense of danger, her regrets, the mistakes she vowed never to repeat. What I know about myself is related to what I know about her, including her secrets, or in some cases fragments of them. I found the pieces both by deliberate effort and by accident, and with each discovery I had to reconfigure the growing whole. (*Fate,* 73–74)

Similar to many first-generation immigrants, John and Daisy Tan held high expectations for their children. Since kindergarten Amy was required not only to achieve academic perfection (i.e., straight A's) but also to practice piano lessons after school. Believing that the brain was the most important part of a person's body, her parents hoped that she would become a neurosurgeon and in her spare time a pianist. Recollecting her mother's instructions, Amy said: "First, if it's too easy, it's not worth pursuing. Second, you have to try harder, no matter what other people might have to do in the same situation—that's your lot in life. And if you're a woman, you're supposed to suffer in silence" (Kepner, 59). Under enormous pressure and moving frequently from one place to another, Amy suffered from loneliness and a strained relationship with her mother in childhood. She found her salvation in books and often turned to them for comfort and joy. As she remembered years later, books were windows opening and illuminating her room when she was young (*Fate*, 1). As a schoolgirl, Amy read classics as well as other books. She identified with Jane Eyre's alienation and her meager hopes, and acquired from Jane Austen's novels "a literary preference for gothic atmosphere and dark emotional resonance" (*Fate*, 221). During her childhood, books were Amy's best friends. Her talent for writing made its appearance quite early. When she was eight years old, her essay on the subject of "What the Library Means to Me" won a prize in a contest sponsored by the Citizens Committee for the Santa Rosa Library and was published in the *Santa Rosa Press Democrat*. Thereafter she secretly harbored the dream of becoming a writer.

During her already difficult adolescence, tragedy in Amy's family greatly increased her sense of loss and confusion. Her elder brother Peter and her father John died from malignant brain tumors just a few months apart in 1967 and 1968. Peter was only sixteen and John, fifty-four. The family was falling apart and Amy, as she described years later, "just kind of went to pieces" (Marvis, 78). Strongly affected by the sudden family losses, her mother Daisy blamed their house for being evil-spirited and decided to take her children Amy and John Jr. away from the wicked influence. The family of three thus traveled first to New York, Washington, and Florida, and then to the Netherlands and Germany before settling down in Switzerland where Daisy rented a place with a beautiful view of the Alps and enrolled Amy and John Jr. in an elite private school. It was during this difficult period of time that Daisy revealed part of her past to Amy and told her about her three daughters from her previous marriage in China.

Amy's life in Europe was filled with a combination of academic success and adolescent rebellion. The already strained relationship between Daisy and Amy deteriorated. After Amy's graduation from the Institut Monte Rosa Internationale, a private boarding school in Montreux, Switzerland, the family of three returned to the United States and settled in the San Francisco area in 1969. Amy enrolled in Linfield College, a conservative Baptist school in McMinnville, Oregon, with an American Baptist Scholarship. She first majored in pre-med studies since Daisy still hoped that her daughter would pursue a medical career as a neurosurgeon. Later Amy transferred first to San Jose City College and then to San Jose State University to be closer to her Italian American boyfriend, Louis M. DeMattei. When Amy changed her major to English and linguistics, the mother-daughter relationship worsened to the point that they completely stopped talking to each other for months. Amy received her bachelor's degree in English and linguistics from San Jose State University in 1973 and her master's degree in linguistics in 1974. In the same year Amy married Louis and started working on her doctorate in linguistics at the University of California at Berkeley.

Two years later, after losing her best friend Peter in a brutal murder, Amy decided to change her life path and left the doctoral program. In 1976, she took a position at the Alameda County Association for Retarded Citizens and began working as a language development specialist for children with speech impediments and learning disabilities. During this period of employment, Amy served as director of a San Francisco project for developmentally handicapped children. Even though Amy was not aware of it at the time, this work experience was valuable later for her life as a writer because she had the opportunity to work with many families with handicapped children and gained priceless knowledge about different kinds of people, families, and relationships. Nevertheless, Amy encountered unexpected difficulty in her job as a language specialist. As E. D. Huntley has pointed out, "As one of the small number of Asian Americans working in language development, and as the sole minority project director for the Bureau of Handicapped Children, Amy soon found herself serving uncomfortably as the representative minority member on various councils and task forces" (7). Feeling unsatisfied with her role in the work place, Amy gave up the administrative job in 1981 and became a reporter for the periodical *Emergency Room Reports* (now *Emergency Medicine Reports*), climbing up the ladder from journalist to the managing editor and associate publisher.

In 1983, Amy became a freelance writer, yet her first territory of exploration was not fiction but business and technical writing. In the next few years, she produced pamphlets, manuals, brochures, business proposals, and other documents for corporations. At the beginning, Amy had only a few small clients, but her skill at handling different kinds of business writing quickly earned her recognition in the field. Unfortunately her success and stable income did not bring happiness to Amy's life. The price she paid for her lucrative business-writing career was long, demanding working hours and a consequent depression that devoured her life and health. Feeling unfulfilled and trapped as an unhappy workaholic, Amy first sought counseling. When such efforts proved in vain, she designed her own therapy, learning to play jazz piano and reading literary works.

Even though Gabriel García Márquez, Raymond Carver, David Leavitt, Richard Ford, and Tobias Wolff's books were on her reading list, most of the texts Amy read during that time were by women writers that included Isabel Allende, Alice Munro, Flannery O'Connor, Amy Hempel, Eudora Welty, Laurie Colwin, Alice Adams, Alice Walker, Lorrie Moore, Anne Tyler, Harriet Doerr, Molly Giles, and Louise Erdrich. Amy later met Amy Hempel, who was very encouraging and gave her helpful advice for a beginning writer (Henderson, 18). Hardly reading any women writers in her college English classes, Amy enjoyed women's works and identified with the sensibility and themes within many of the novels and short stories. In particular, the Native American family tales portrayed in Louise Erdrich's *Love Medicine* (1984) had a profound influence on her. She started to comprehend different ways of telling stories and writing fiction. At the time, she did not realize that these readings would change her life path in a dramatic way.

Amy's short story "Endgame," later retitled "Rules of the Game," earned her a pass to join the Squaw Valley Community of Writers, directed by the novelist Oakley Maxwell Hall, author of *The Art and Craft of Novel Writing* (1989) and *How Fiction Works* (2000). This story was later incorporated into her debut novel *The Joy Luck Club*. It has been collected in such literary anthologies as *Growing up Ethnic in America: Contemporary Fiction about Learning to be American* (1999) and *Big City Cool: Short Stories about Urban Youth* (2002). It also has been used as a sample short story for English, writing, and literature classes to teach students critical thinking and writing skills. Robert DiYanni's *Literature: Approaches to Fiction, Poetry, and Drama* (2008), for example, includes the story "Rules of the Game" in the section on fiction. Initially hoping to learn about writing techniques and character development in the Squaw Valley workshop, Amy did not realize at the time how much this experience would benefit her future career as a fiction writer. Through this workshop Amy met her friend and mentor Molly Giles, an award-winning fiction writer who introduced Amy to her long-term literary agent and friend Sandra Dijkstra. After this workshop, Molly Giles led another writers' workshop in San Francisco that continued to provide a nourishing environment for new writers like Amy Tan.

In 1987 Amy and Louis accompanied Daisy to China where Amy finally met two of her half sisters. Before that trip, Amy had sent her agent three stories together with an outline for a collection that she titled

Wind and Water. Sandra Dijkstra managed to negotiate a contract and a $50,000 advance with G. P. Putnam's Sons, quite an impressive deal for a first book. After she returned from China, Amy closed her freelance writing business and became a full-time fiction writer. She turned to writing every day in her study in the basement, listening to the Japanese music of Kitaro, and burning incense sticks to create an atmosphere "that spurred her imagination and helped her to focus her mind on the task at hand" (Darraj, 60). In this setting, Amy wrote the other thirteen stories and finished the whole book within a few months.

Retitled *The Joy Luck Club*, a name suggested by Dijkstra, the collection of stories was published as a novel in 1989. Its immediate success surprised many, including Amy Tan herself. Reflecting on her busy schedule for book signings, speeches, lectures, and other activities to promote her first novel, she states, "the word *author* is as chilling as rigor mortis, and I shudder when I hear myself introduced as such" (*Fate,* 7; italics in the original). Her well-received first book enabled Amy to enter the American literary landscape as a rising star. Louise Erdrich's words of endorsement on the book jacket read: "Amy effortlessly mixes tenderness and bitter irony, sorrow and slicing wit. *The Joy Luck Club* is a fabulous concoction" (Darraj, 62). For Amy, writing *The Joy Luck Club* was an exploration of the tensions and bonds she and her mother experienced for years. "When I was writing, it was so much for my mother and myself," as Amy put it. "I wanted her to know what I thought about China and what I thought about growing up in this country" (Lew, 23). The emotions, story line, and characters strike a chord in many readers' hearts.

In the heated debate over cultural authenticity in Asian American literary studies, *The Joy Luck Club* has been cited frequently. Frank Chin, in his essay "Come All Ye Asian American Writers of the Real and the Fake," for example, condemned Amy Tan together with Maxine Hong Kingston and David Henry Hwang for faking the Chinese and Chinese American tradition in order to win applause from the American mainstream. Elaine H. Kim, however, favored Amy's first novel as a "story of how women's lives flow through each other—whether mothers and daughters, friends and relations, rich girls and beggar girls, or sisters across oceans and continent" (83). Aside from occasional criticism, *The Joy Luck Club* received overwhelming praise among general readers, critics, and literary scholars.

Following the great success of *The Joy Luck Club* came Amy's "angst of the second book." Like many other writers, writing the "doomed" second book became a painstaking process. She started and then discarded several story lines, which accumulated to about one thousand pages by her count, before returning to her main source of inspiration—her mother Daisy's life. Amy's second novel, *The Kitchen God's Wife,* dismissed the doubts of many critics and readers and confirmed her talent for fiction writing. A story based on Daisy's disastrous first marriage as well as her life in war-torn China and then the United States, Amy's second novel became a best seller shortly after its publication in 1991 and received mostly positive reviews all over the country.

By 2008 Amy Tan had published three more novels: *The Hundred Secret Senses* (1995), *The Bonesetter's Daughter* (2001), and *Saving Fish from Drowning* (2005); a collection of nonfiction, *The Opposite of Fate: A Book of Musings* (2003); and two children's books in collaboration with her friend Gretchen Schields, *The Moon Lady* (1992) and *The Chinese Siamese Cat* (1994). In addition, she has collaborated in writing a screenplay, a stage play script, and an opera libretto, and is the author of several essays and short stories. She has appeared frequently in interviews on radio and television programs, and has given speeches and talks around the country and abroad. References to her life and writing are abundant in print sources as well as on the Internet. Her works remain a staple of school curricula and classroom and book club reading lists. She is certainly one of the most popular contemporary American writers.

Her successful writing career has brought Amy Tan many honors. She was conferred an honorary Doctorate of Humane Letters from Dominican College in San Rafael, California, in 1991 and an honorary Doctoral Degree of Letters from Simmons College in Boston, Massachusetts, in 2003. She received a Writer for Writers Award acknowledging her assistance to young authors in 2003. Besides the prestigious literary awards and nominations bestowed on her works, she also has been recognized for her achievement as a Chinese American. In 2000 Amy was honored by the Museum of Chinese in America for her contribution to the preservation of Chinese American history and promoting public awareness of Chinese American experience and community (Snodgrass, 25). Her book-length biography is included in the Chelsea House series "Asian Americans of Achievement" among other notables such as Daniel Inouye, Michelle Kwan, Maya Lin, Yo-Yo Ma, Vera Wang, and Kristi Yamaguchi.

Although the narratives and characters in Amy Tan's works are not strictly autobiographical, her family history and personal life inspire her writing, filter through her fiction, and leave abundant traces. As the first American-born generation in an immigrant family, Amy experienced typical struggles over assimilation and cultural identity in her childhood and young adulthood. Her mother's eccentric beliefs and dramatic behaviors further worsened the situation. For a long time, Amy blamed her unhappiness on her Chinese heritage and her mother. As a child and a teenager, Amy shunned Chinese culture and strived to achieve complete assimilation without realizing how much her Chinese American heritage would profoundly affect her life and writing career.

Looking back, Amy considers her childhood "too full of coincidences, too full of melodrama, veering toward the implausible in both tragedy and comedy," but she believes her life is "excellent fodder for fiction" (*Fate*, 33). Well known for her compelling fiction that captures the emotional tension and complexity between Chinese immigrant mothers and their American-born daughters, Amy Tan's relationship to her own mother was strained from early on. Years later in an interview, she described herself as "a gloomy kid" who began to have thoughts of suicide at the age of six and fought almost every day with her mother from the age of eight ("Amy Tan Biography: A Uniquely Personal Storyteller"). The final reconciliation of their emotional turmoil did not come until Daisy was hospitalized for a suspected heart attack in 1985 while Amy was on vacation in Hawaii. Even though it turned out to be merely an episode of angina, Amy was shocked and promised to learn more about her mother. In her last few years of life Daisy suffered from Alzheimer's disease and passed away on November 22, 1999, surrounded by loved ones. For Amy, writing is the means through which she connects with her mother, her grandmother, and the past. It is "an act of faith," a hope that she discovers the meaning of truth (*Fate*, 323). As she puts it:

> In my writing room, I go back into the past, to that moment when my grandmother told my mother not to follow her footsteps. My grandmother and I are walking side by side, imagining the past differently, remembering it another way. Together we come upon a tomb of memories. We open it and release what has been buried for too long—the terrible despair, the destructive rage. We hurt, we grieve, we cry. And then we see what remains: the hopes, broken to bits but still there. (*Fate*, 104)

As a writer, Amy Tan continues to explore new territories after the overwhelming success of her debut novel. In her words, "I kept searching for this thing, this click that would make me feel I had finally done enough—either the right project or working hard enough or earning enough money or feeling that I had written the best thing" (Somogyi and Stanton, 27). Perhaps nobody has summarized Amy's life and writing career better than herself:

> I have qualities in my nature shaped by my past—a secret legacy of suicide, forced marriages, and abandoned children in China; an eclectic upbringing that included no fewer than fifteen

residences, ranging from tough neighborhoods in Oakland, California, to the snobbish environs of Montreux, Switzerland; a distorted view of life shaped by two conflicting religions, the death of my father and brother in a year's time, and the murder of my best friend. Those elements and others in my life have combined to make me feel that writing provides the sort of freedom and danger, satisfaction and discomfort, truth and contradiction that I can't find anywhere else in life. (*Fate*, 321–22)

This is Amy Tan who writes for herself, her mother, and many others.

DISCUSSION QUESTIONS

- Compare the mother-daughter relationships between the four pairs of mothers and daughters in *The Joy Luck Club*. What are the similarities and what are the differences? To what extent do these relationships resemble Amy Tan's relationships with her mother Daisy?
- Compare the generational conflicts depicted in *The Joy Luck Club* and *The Bonesetter's Daughter*. What do the characters share in common and what are their major distinctions? What do they tell us about the common threads and changes in Amy Tan's writing?
- In *The Hundred Secret Senses*, Amy Tan portrays a sisterly bond. What do you think makes this novel a thematic departure from her earlier works, *The Joy Luck Club* and *The Kitchen God's Wife*? And, what important themes are carried on in this third novel?
- *Saving Fish from Drowning* tells the story of a group of American tourists in Burma. Discuss the change of characters, themes, and settings in this book, compared to Tan's earlier novels.

2

AMY TAN AND THE NOVEL
AND SHORT STORY

Appearing on the contemporary American literary horizon as a fiction writer and novelist, Amy Tan is well known for her engaging and thought-provoking stories, remarkable characters, rich imagery, and unique language style. *Newsweek* called her "one of the prime story-tellers writing fiction today … with a rare power to touch the heart" (Kort, 212). Tan holds a place in Asian American as well as contemporary American literature mainly due to her intriguing storytelling "which enriches the genre of fiction in its explorations of the connection between past and present and her characters' struggles over family relations and identity construction" (Dong, 2131). For Tan, storytelling is an inheritance she received from her family as well as a gift she presents to her readers. Addressing her inspiration, Tan often credits her parents:

> I think that I got the storytelling primarily from my father, as much as from my mother…. He was a Baptist minister and his idea of quality time with his children—since he worked seven days a week—was to read his sermons aloud to me and see what I thought and if there were any words I didn't under-stand. His sermons were like stories; they were very personable. Stories from my mother came more naturally, and I'd listen as she and my aunts sat a table covered with newspapers, shelling

fava beans or chopping vegetables and gossiping about the
family, and going on for hours and hours about some little
detail that they found disgusting in some relative or friend.
(Giles)

To Tan, storytelling enriches her writing career on different levels. A
skillful storyteller, Tan writes novels and short stories in such engaging
ways that they appeal to a broad range of readers regardless of their cultural background. Commenting on the universal appeal of her works,
Tan has said:

> I think that the other reason that I've become a storyteller is
> that I was raised with so many different conflicting ideas that it
> posed many questions for me in life, and those questions
> became a filter for looking at all my experiences and seeing
> them from different angles. That's what I think that a story-
> teller does, and underneath the surface of the story is a ques-
> tion or a perspective or a nagging little emotion, and then it
> grows. (Giles)

More often than not, readers of Tan's novels are led to contemplate
the questions, ideas, and perspectives embedded in her touching stories.
Storytelling is also a key process for Tan's characters to "revitalize a past
that is significant in the creation of the identity of ethnic groups in
America" (López Morell, 84). Many of Tan's Chinese American characters are adept storytellers who present charming narratives naturally. In
addition, by passing on the stories of the past, the older generation provides the younger generation with the "necessary roots to feel powerful"
and to mend generational gaps (López Morell, 84). Particularly in Tan's
early publications, generational bondings as well as conflicts are woven
into the complex narratives.

NARRATIVE STRUCTURE

In her fiction, Tan seldom utilizes a linear narrative. Instead, she tells
her stories in an intricate structure in which the past and present are
intertwined. Tan called the structure of her first novel the result of "a
more eclectic arrangement of sixteen *short stories*" (Tan, *The Opposite
of Fate*, 304; italics in the original). Labeled as her "first work of fiction" by Tan's publisher with her consent, the sixteen stories are self-
contained and at the same time "connected by theme or emotion or

community" (Somogyi and Stanton, 26). Many reviewers, critics, and literary students have strived to decipher the innovative structure of *The Joy Luck Club* in a variety of ways. Zenobia Mistri called Tan's book a "short story sequence" whose structure is a "central metaphor for the thematic elements that link those stories to each other, involving an implicit conversation among the four mothers and their daughters as they tell their stories" (251, 252). Together the stories capture "the neurotic comedy of contemporary life styles and the scarring tragedies of the hidden Chinese past" (Rubin, 13) while comprising the author's dedication to her mother and the memory of her grandmother.

Another innovative aspect of *The Joy Luck Club* is that the novel includes multiple first-person narratives that not only help organize the numerous events scattered across temporal and geographical lines, but also provide differing perspectives. In focusing on "many singular 'I's," the novel is engaged in experiential transformation and "ultimately reconfigures a Chinese-American identity that is a well-balanced ethnic bipolarity in a diasporic individual" (Zeng, 7). The characters' decentered and multi-perspective first-person accounts contribute to "a tradition of multiple monologue narratives" that includes prestigious literary names such as Virginia Woolf, William Faulkner, Louise Erdrich, Peter Matthiessen, Louis Auchincloss, and Kaye Gibbons (Souris, 99). Thus the narrative segments in *The Joy Luck Club* are connected thematically; collectively they provide diverse voices and vantage points.

Besides the vivid characters and engaging story lines, Tan's novels are praised for their cultural and historical representations. In *The Joy Luck Club*, for example, the characters' personal narratives are closely tied to the historical and cultural contexts of China and Chinese America. Walter Shear praises the novel's structure as a success "in manifesting not merely the individual psychic tragedies of those caught up in this history, but the enormous agony of a culture enmeshed in a transforming crisis" (193). Such a narrative structure reminds readers of literary works such as Sherwood Anderson's *Winesburg, Ohio* (1919), Ernest Hemingway's *In Our Time* (1925), and William Faulkner's *The Unvanquished* (1938), "books that feature distinct, individual narratives but that as a group simultaneously dramatize the panorama of a critical transition in cultural values" (Shear, 193). With the shifting space and time, the reader observes and feels the characters' experiences as the plot develops.

Catherine Romagnolo has examined Tan's novel with a particular focus on narrative beginnings from a feminist perspective. Romagnolo applies four categories (structural narrative openings, chronological narrative beginnings, causal beginnings, and thematic origins) to analyze the narrative structure as well as cultural themes of Tan's book. Her study indicates that *The Joy Luck Club* provides a unique case for narrative study in contemporary literature.

As a writer, Tan keeps on exploring new narrative structures. Different from *The Joy Luck Club*, her second novel, *The Kitchen God's Wife* adopts a structure of a story within a story. The book is told almost entirely by the mother character, Winnie Louie, and utilizes the brief narratives of the daughter, Pearl Louie Brandt, as bookends. *The Hundred Secret Senses* weaves together the previous lives of Miss Nelly Banner and Nunumu in nineteenth-century China and the current lives of Olivia Bishop and Kwan Li in contemporary San Francisco in an intricate structure which unfolds the family secrets and connections between characters gradually. *The Bonesetter's Daughter*, in contrast, shifts the focus from using storytelling as an oral genre to women's writing as a way to reveal generational bonds and family relations. Tan's novel *Saving Fish from Drowning* is a breakthrough in terms of narrative structure, characters, and subject matters, and reflects the author's continuous exploration in fiction writing.

FICTION, HISTORY, MEMORY

Tan has been recognized as a contemporary American writer who crafts novels "that resist facile and definitive classification into any of the conventional fictional genres" (Huntley, 19). Her insightful and creative storytelling incorporates a combination of elements from "biography and autobiography, history and folk tale, memory and imagination" (Dong, 2131). In this sense, Tan explores a new possibility for fiction narrative and enriches the generic tradition of novel writing.

In Tan's novels, her characters' personal stories are often interwoven with their social and cultural contexts; as a result, fiction, history, and memory are blended together seamlessly. Such impeccable mixture enables the reader to enjoy the life stories of the characters and at the same time to ask meaningful questions about the cultural context. By incorporating her family history and personal experience into her novels, Tan writes powerful fiction. Her grandmother and mother's lives, in particular, inspired stories in *The Joy Luck Club* and *The Kitchen God's Wife*. In Tan's understanding, "characters are subconsciously linked to things you know intimately. I have a headstrong side and a passive side; I think I took these different sides of my mother and myself and explored. I was very conscious of trying to understand my different character traits" (Henderson, 20). For her, writing from memory is about remembering her psychological place in the world at different stages of her life and remembering her evolving sense of life. Such subjective memory is "simultaneously the most unreliable *and* the most authentic element a writer can infuse into her work" (*Fate*, 110; italics in the original). In drawing on memory that is cultural, familial, and personal, Tan develops her imagination into endless possibilities in fiction writing.

Even though Tan's early novels feature Chinese and Chinese American main characters whose stories provide a glimpse into particular cultural and historical contexts of China (for example, war-torn China during the 1930s and 1940s) and of Chinese America (for instance, San Francisco in the 1960s and 1970s), they also raise meaningful questions on a more universal level, such as the themes of family, love, and life. Through her characters' memory, recollection, and reflection, Tan presents their life stories in an engaging way. In reflecting on her writing of *The Kitchen God's Wife* as a fiction of her mother's story, Tan gave her insight on the genre: "I changed her story.... And yet it is as close to the truth as I can imagine. It is my mother's story in the most important of ways to me: her passion, her will, her hope, the innocence she never really lost. It is the reason why she told me, 'I was not affected,' why I can finally understand what she truly meant" (*Fate*, 211).

Tan's novels usually have close ties to certain historical contexts and therefore lend themselves readily to the study of historical literature. *The Kitchen God's Wife*, for example, set during the Japanese invasion and occupation of China in the 1930s and 1940s, raises questions about how to understand fact and fiction in historical literature. In *The Kitchen God's Wife*, to use Gayatri Spivak's words, "fiction is also historical" and "history is also fictive" (Adams, 2003, 11). Tan's novel interweaves historical narratives with personal stories. In this sense, she is among the contemporary writers who explore new possibilities in fiction writing.

ASIAN AMERICAN WRITING

In praising *The Joy Luck Club*, Orville Schell remarked that by writing about the experience of being caught between countries and cultures, "writers such as Maxine Hong Kingston and now Amy Tan have begun to create what is, in effect, a new genre of American fiction" (3). Earning her literary reputation with *The Woman Warrior: Memoirs of a Girlhood among Ghosts* (1976), Kingston has helped introduce Asian American literature to a mainstream audience. "Her innovative writing has demonstrated the possibility to redefine memoirs and fiction through creating an invented form of narrative, empowered by elements of history, biography, memory, legend, folktale, myth, and anecdote" (Dong c, 1251).

Kingston's writing has inspired and paved the way for younger generations of writers, including Amy Tan. In her compelling storytelling, Tan successfully intertwines various elements and examines such complicated issues as identity, the immigrant experience, family, and love, among others. "In Tan's hands, these linked stories—diverse as they are—fit almost magically into a powerfully coherent novel, whose winning combination of ingredients—immigrant experience, mother-daughter ties, Pacific Rim culture—make it a book with the 'good luck' to be in the right place at the right time" (Rubin, 13). The complexity and multiplicity of Tan's novels have added a new dimension to contemporary American fiction.

A number of scholars have discussed the tradition of "talk-story" underscored in many Chinese American women's works, including those of Kingston and Tan. Karen Kai-Yuan Su, for example, wrote her doctoral dissertation about Asian American women's writing focusing on Jade Snow Wong's *Fifth Chinese Daughter* (1950), Kingston's *The Woman Warrior*, and Tan's *The Joy Luck Club*. Lisa M. S. Dunick points to the significance of women's writing when discussing Tan's *The Bonesetter's Daughter*. Women's storytelling and writing in Tan's fiction gives Chinese and Chinese American women a voice in contemporary literature.

Young Adult Literature

According to Frances A. Nadeau's 1995 article "The Mother/Daughter Relationship in Young Adult Fiction," when Tan published her first novel, few authors described the complex mother-daughter relationship in their works for young adults. In this sense, Tan has led the way for other writers. At the end of her article that provides a context for reading *The Joy Luck Club* as young adult literature, Nadeau includes an annotated list of books introducing other important works for young adults such as Fran Arrick's *Nice Girl from Good Home* (1984), A. E. Cannon's *Amazing Gracie* (1991), Sook Nyul Choi's *Echoes of the White Giraffe* (1993), Pam Conrad's *Taking the Ferry Home* (1988), and Sarah Ellis's *Pick-Up Sticks* (1992), among others.

Judith Hayn and Deborah Sherrill's article, "Female Protagonists in Multicultural Young Adult Literature: Sources and Strategies," identifies two novels by Tan that are often read in high school classes (*The Joy Luck Club* and *The Kitchen God's Wife*) featuring female characters and Chinese American families. This again confirms not only Tan's popularity and importance among young adult readers, but also the usefulness of her works for educational purposes.

BEYOND GENRE

Tan has compared her writing process to dreaming: "I have found in dreams that I can change the setting by simply looking down at my feet then looking up again. I'll be following my feet for a while and, if I don't like what I see in front of me, I will just look down at my feet. I'll start walking, and when I look up, I'll be in a different place" (Tan, "Amy Tan," in *Writer's Dreaming*, 284). In the realm of fiction writing, Tan often explores different literary territories. The best example might be *Saving Fish from Drowning*, in which she uses fictional devices from a number of genres: murder mystery, romance, picaresque, comic novel, magical realism, fable, myth, police detective, political farce, and so forth (http://amytan.net).

It might strike some readers as an odd juxtaposition that Tan combines comic and romantic styles with the repressive political situation of Burma in *Saving Fish from Drowning*. For Tan, nonetheless, "humor and fiction are among the most potent ways to address serious problems and keep people's attention on it" (http://amytan.net). Writing with both entertainment and seriousness in mind, Tan has presented another interesting novel for readers to enjoy while they discover the embedded political messages.

DISCUSSION QUESTIONS

- Many readers and critics have found similarities between Amy Tan's life and her writing in *The Joy Luck Club*. To what extent is her fiction autobiographical? How does this difference from conventional fiction affect the reader's reading experience and their understanding of contemporary American literature?
- *The Kitchen God's Wife* is based on the life experience of Tan's mother, Daisy. To what extent is the novel biographical and autobiographical? How does her use of real-life events in this novel differ from that in *The Joy Luck Club*?
- Tan considers *The Bonesetter's Daughter* her most personal publication. Discuss how the novel relates to the author's life experience, and how she follows or violates the generic conventions of fiction.
- Discuss Tan's influence on contemporary American fiction in general and Asian American fiction in particular.

- Do you consider *The Opposite of Fate* to be Tan's memoir? Why or why not? What does this book share in common with or do differently from conventional memoirs?
- In a number of ways, *Saving Fish from Drowning* shows a change of direction from Tan's earlier works. Discuss the specific distinctions of this novel compared to her earlier ones.

3

THE JOY LUCK CLUB
(1989)

The Joy Luck Club was first published in hardcover in 1989 by G. P. Putnam's Sons. Later Amy Tan received a considerable amount from Vintage-Random House for the paperback rights (Lew, 23). Tan's debut novel has sold over four million paperback copies and over 275,000 hardcover copies (Wong, 174), and has been translated into more than twenty languages, including Chinese. The novel received predominantly favorable reviews and won a series of honors after its publication, including: nomination for the *Los Angeles Times* Book Award, finalist for the National Book Award and the National Book Critics Circle Award, winner of the Bay Area Book Reviewers Award for Best Fiction, winner of the Commonwealth Club Gold Award, and winner of the American Library Association Best Book for Young Adults Award. It climbed onto the *New York Times* hardcover best sellers list about a month after its publication and remained on the list for nine months, and is still a frequent title on reading lists for high school and college courses and among book clubs. Page numbers cited from *The Joy Luck Club* in this chapter are from the 1989 paperback edition (New York: Ivy Books, the Random House Publishing Group).

PLOT SUMMARY

Published as a novel, *The Joy Luck Club* includes sixteen interrelated stories of four pairs of mothers and daughters: Suyuan and Jing-mei (June)
Woo, An-mei Hsu and Rose Hsu Jordan, Lindo and Waverly Jong, and
Ying-ying and Lena St. Clair. Narrated by different characters in the first
person, the stories are divided into four sections: "Feathers from a Thousand Li Away," "The Twenty-Six Malignant Gates," "American Translation," and "Queen Mother of the Western Skies." Each section includes
four stories, introduced by a vignette with embedded metaphorical meanings. The stories of the mother and daughter characters are intertwined.
The personal narratives by multiple narrators cover a number of different
places and times. In the process, the plot is developed thematically. At
once a collection of short stories and a coherent novel, *The Joy Luck Club*
challenges the conventional understanding of both genres.

The book begins with Jing-mei's narrative. Titled "The Joy Luck
Club," the first chapter is set in San Francisco two months after Jing-
mei's mother, Suyuan, died of a cerebral aneurysm. Because of her mother's sudden death, Jing-mei is expected to replace her as the fourth
corner on the mah jong table at the next Joy Luck Club gathering as
well as take care of Suyuan's unfinished business. Jing-mei's voice tells
how her mother initiated the Joy Luck Club in Kweilin, China, during
the Japanese invasion. At the time, four young women would take turns
hosting mah jong games. They served and consumed any food that they
could manage to find and told stories about good times in the past and
hopes for the future. Such gatherings during wartime helped raise their
spirits despite the fear, despair, and miseries of the real world. After
immigrating to the United States, Suyuan started the San Francisco version of the Joy Luck Club in 1949, when she met An-mei Hsu, Lindo
Jong, and Ying-ying St. Clair at the First Chinese Baptist Church.
Besides mah jong and food, their Club activities over the years have been
occupied by their memories of China and by their American-born children. Jing-mei's narrative that opens the novel introduces a number of
story lines that the rest of the book will unfold: Jing-mei's recollection of
her childhood and often strained relationship with her mother, her
upcoming trip to China and meeting with her twin half sisters, and the
life experiences of each Joy Luck Club aunt in China and the United
States and their relationships with their American-born daughters. The
first chapter is also of particular importance in organizing the whole
book thematically and in establishing bridges among the stories.

Through Jing-mei's framing narrative, *The Joy Luck Club* covers a
long time span from the 1930s to the 1980s and different geographical
locations in China and the United States. Thematically interrelated, the

chapters allow each character to tell her story in a first-person narrative, except for Suyuan whose story is told in Jing-mei's voice. The mother characters' voices relate their life in China from childhood to adulthood as well as their experience as immigrants in the United States. The daughters' stories portray their childhood struggles with identity and parental expectations together with the issues of their personal lives: Jing-mei, unmarried at the age of thirty-six, is trying to advance her career in freelance business writing; Rose is getting a divorce after years of being unable to make decisions; a divorcée, Waverly struggles to find a way to tell her mother about her engagement to her Caucasian fiancé; and Lena feels trapped in a powerless position in her marriage that is supposedly based on "equality." Facing difficulties in their current lives, the daughters have the opportunity to revisit their (dis)connections with their mothers. Through these interconnected episodes, the book depicts the complex relationships between the mothers and daughters: their misunderstandings, their cultural and generational differences, as well as their love and bonds. As the stories progress, each mother-daughter pair gains understanding and eventually comes to reconciliation.

The book ends with the chapter "A Pair of Tickets" narrated by Jing-mei. On her first trip to China, Jing-mei visited her father's hometown Guangzhou with her seventy-two-year-old father, Canning Woo. It was in China that Jing-mei finally found out how her mother had to leave her twin babies on the road when she fled from Kweilin to Chungking in order to escape the invading Japanese troops. At the time, Suyuan was certain she was going to die soon and decided to leave the babies on the roadside with all her valuables and her picture in the hope that other people might save them. Found and raised by a peasant couple, Wei Han and Wei Ching, the twins grew up knowing their birth mother from the picture. The book closes with the reunion of Jing-mei and her half sisters, Chwun Yu and Chwun Hwa, for whom Suyuan had been searching for years. At the airport in Shanghai, Jing-mei finally understood her mother's love and hope for her. Standing together the three sisters all saw it: "Together we look like our mother. Her same eyes, her same mouth, open in surprise to see, at last, her long-cherished wish" (*Club*, 332).

CHARACTERS, THEMES, AND SETTINGS

Well known for her insightful portrayal of the mother-daughter bond, Tan's novel features four pairs of mothers and daughters as the main characters. Through the multiple narrators, the novel depicts different settings in a number of Chinese cities (Kweilin, Chungking, Shanghai, Wushi, Taiyuan, and others) as well as in San Francisco where the four families live at the present time.

The character Jing-mei Woo provides the framing narrative for the whole book and plays a significant role in connecting all the stories. Jing-mei grew up with a mother who believed people could be anything they wanted in America and who projected her hopes on her American-born daughter. Suyuan Woo is "absent" when the story begins in the 1980s in San Francisco, a couple of months after her death. Her life story is thus narrated in Jing-mei's voice. Born in China, Suyuan was first married to Wang Fuchi, an officer with the Kuomintang, and had twin girls. When the Japanese troops invaded China in the 1930s, Suyuan moved to Kweilin and then to Chungking in order to join her husband and to run away from the Japanese soldiers. After fleeing Kweilin on foot, Suyuan had to abandon her belongings one after another and was delirious. She could not bear to watch her babies die with her. Hence, she left them when she was certain that she would die of dysentery, or from starvation, or from the Japanese who were marching closely behind her. After her miraculous survival and arrival in Chungking, Suyuan found out that her husband had already died. She met Canning Woo in the hospital and started searching for her daughters immediately. After immigrating to the United States in 1949 and settling down in San Francisco, Suyuan and Canning had a daughter and named her Jing-mei, meaning "pure essence, younger sister." Even after leaving China, Suyuan never gave up hope of finding her other daughters. When communication resumed between China and the United States, Suyuan immediately contacted old friends in Shanghai and Kweilin, continuing her search. It took years before one of her schoolmates found the twins. Sadly, Suyuan's unexpected death deprived her of the last chance to meet her grown daughters. Tan named the character of the mother "Suyuan," meaning "long-cherished wish" in Chinese. Suyuan's wish would be fulfilled by the reunion of her three daughters—Jing-mei, Chwun Yu, and Chwun Hwa—as well as their final understanding of her motherly love and hope.

In many ways, Suyuan and Jing-mei's relationship echoes the bond between many mothers and daughters, immigrants or otherwise. Jing-mei often feels that her mother does not understand her and has unrealistic expectations for her. As a result, she feels like a failure who is unable to meet her mother's high expectations on many different occasions. In Jing-mei's memory, her mother made continuous efforts to shape her into a child prodigy; modeling her after Shirley Temple and making her practice piano lessons were just a couple of examples out of many. As Jing-mei remembers, she failed her mother again and again while growing up and Suyuan's disappointment devastated Jing-mei. It was not until after Suyuan's death that Jing-mei would play her piano again and find how easily the notes came back to her. As the novel shows in a subtle way, Suyuan knew her daughter well and loved her deeply. At the last New Year's dinner, for example, Suyuan knew ahead of time that Jing-mei would be the only person to pick up the steamed crab with a missing leg while others would choose the plumpest and brightest ones. In trying to figure out the meaning of her "life's importance" (i.e., a jade pendant on a gold chain that her mother gave her shortly before her death), Jing-mei came to understand her mother and their relationship. The jade pendant symbolizes Jing-mei's trait inherited from her mother. After all, Suyuan saw the "best quality" in her daughter all these years and her hopes were an embodiment of her motherly love.

In her essay "Mother Tongue," first delivered in 1989 at the conference "The State of the English Language," Amy Tan talked about her unique writing style in *The Joy Luck Club*. This essay was published in *The Threepenny Review*, then anthologized in *The Best American Essays 1991*, and later collected in *The Opposite of Fate*. In it Tan confessed her initial effort to write her fiction using "big" English words in order to form a sophisticated style before resorting to the everyday language she used with her mother since childhood.

> I later decided I should envision a reader for the stories I would write. And the reader I decided on was my mother, because these were stories about mothers. So with this reader in mind—and in fact she did read my early drafts—I began to write stories using all the Englishes I grew up with: the English I spoke to my mother, which for lack of a better term might be described as "simple"; the English she used with me, which for lack of a better term might be described as "broken"; my translation of her Chinese, which could certainly be described as "watered down"; and what I imagined to be her translation of her Chinese if she could speak in perfect English, her internal language, and for that I sought to preserve the essence, but neither an English nor a Chinese structure. (*The Opposite of Fate*, 278-279)

Adopting such a language style, Tan hoped to capture her mother's intent, passion, imagery, the rhythms of her speech, and the nature of her thoughts. Tan was quite proud of achieving her goal when her mother Daisy told her *The Joy Luck Club* was "[s]o easy to read" (*Fate*, 279). As a matter of fact, Tan's unique language style has won approval not only from her mother but also from many reviewers, critics, and readers.

The story of An-mei Hsu is heavily based on the life experiences of Tan's mother and grandmother. In the novel, An-mei relates her childhood from 1923 in Ningbo, China. Her father had passed away and An-mei and her younger brother were living in her uncle and aunt's house with their maternal grandmother. An-mei's mother had become the fourth wife of a rich merchant and thus was such a disgraced outcast in her own family that speaking her name was forbidden. When her grandmother fell sick, nine-year-old An-mei witnessed how her mother came back home as an unwelcome guest and cut a piece of flesh from the softest part of her arm and put it into a soup to try to save her. After the grandmother's funeral, An-mei followed her mother to Tientsin to live in the household of Wu Tsing, a man who raped her mother and forced her to become one of his concubines. It was in Wu's huge house that An-mei uncovered the truth of her mother's unhappy life and the nature of Wu's other wives. After An-mei's mother gave birth to a baby boy, Wu Tsing's only male heir, the second wife claimed the child and further devastated the unfortunate concubine. As a child, An-mei watched her mother die from swallowing raw opium wrapped in sticky sweet dumplings two days before the Lunar New Year. Her suicide right before the New Year made Wu Tsing fearful of her vengeful spirit. Wu Tsing promised to take good care of An-mei and her baby brother. In sacrificing her own life, her mother gave An-mei strength and hope. An-mei later married George Hsu; they had seven children in America: Rose, Ruth, Janice, Matthew, Mark, Luke, and Bing.

Years after her mother's death, An-mei found it ironic that even though she tried to raise her daughter Rose differently from herself, she still came out the same. In the 1980s, Rose was in the middle of a divorce. She was married, against the will of both families, to Ted Jordan, a dermatologist from a wealthy family. Looking back, Rose realized that her relationship with Ted fell into an unfortunate pattern from the very beginning: he was the hero who made all the decisions and she was the victim who followed him around without question. Her inability to take action and to find her voice led to her present unhappy life. Going through such a difficult time in her personal life gave Rose a chance to revisit her bond with her mother. When Rose eventually stood up for herself, as An-mei hoped, she not only saved herself from misery but also came closer to her mother in her heart.

Lindo Jong's story starts with her memory of a childhood in Taiyuan. She was engaged at the age of two to Tyan-yu Huang, a one-year-old boy, by arrangement of the village matchmaker. Since then, even though she lived with her own family for the next ten years, she was treated like an outsider. Yet, she could feel her mother's love deeply. Losing most of their property in a flood, Lindo's family had to go to Wushi and seek refuge with a relative. As a result, Lindo had to move to her in-laws' house when she was twelve. In the Huangs' courtyard stood a four-story building that housed the four generations of the family. In this household Lindo served her mother-in-law and future husband obediently like a servant for four years before the wedding ceremony took place when she was sixteen. However, her service could not satisfy her mother-in-law because she failed to provide an heir to the Huang family. Lindo's young husband was deep down still a boy and they shared a bed like brother and sister. Her miserable life with the Huangs continued until Lindo tricked her mother-in-law, escaped from the marriage, and made her way first to Beijing and then to America. Through An-mei, Lindo met and later married Tin Jong. They had three children: Winston, Vincent, and Waverly.

Since girlhood, Lindo had a determined and strong-willed character. Such characteristics were passed on to her American-born daughter, Waverly. The story narrated by Waverly, "Rules of the Game," was originally published on its own as a short story. In her narrative, Waverly recollects her experience of becoming a child chess prodigy after learning "the art of invisible strength" from her mother. Even though Waverly enjoyed a period of triumph in chess games, she lost her strength after she confronted her mother because Lindo was bragging about her. After that Waverly lost her chess games and stopped playing entirely. Very much like her mother, Waverly also had manipulative aspects and uncanny abilities. After divorcing her Chinese American husband Marvin Chen, Waverly became a tax attorney. Their daughter Shoshana lives with Waverly. In the present, Waverly is having a hard time breaking the news to her overly critical mother that she is getting married to Rich Schields, a Caucasian tax attorney. Set between Waverly's engagement and wedding, Lindo and Waverly's narratives connect the past with the present and help the mother and daughter to mend their relationship and realize how much they resemble and love each other.

Compared to Lindo, Ying-ying St. Clair is a more introspective character who keeps her feelings and thoughts hidden. Her story begins in the autumn of 1918 in Wushi when four-year-old Ying-ying was lost and found during the Moon Festival. (Tan later developed this episode into a children's book, *The Moon Lady*, illustrated by her good friend Gretchen Schields.) Born into one of the richest families in Wushi, Ying-ying grew up a wild and stubborn child. After she naively married an unfaithful man at the age of sixteen, Ying-ying started to taste the bitterness of life. After being abandoned by her husband, Ying-ying spent years in solitude in a relative's house in the countryside before she returned to the city and took a job as a shop girl. It was in Shanghai that Ying-ying met Clifford St. Clair, an American exporter. He courted her for four years before she finally agreed to marry him, even though she did not love him. A lonely character in America, Ying-ying communicated with her English-speaking husband in gestures, looks, moods, and her very limited English. After her second baby was stillborn, Ying-ying fell apart, piece by piece. As a result of her mother's depression, Lena's childhood was filled with confusion and fear.

Lena St. Clair, daughter of a Chinese mother and an English-Irish father, shared her mother's sense of being "lost" and "displaced." In her relationship with Harold Livotny, Lena always fell into a powerless position. Even though she was the one to encourage Harold to start running his own business in restaurant design and development, she became just an associate for Livotny & Associates while Harold became a partner. Her creative ideas helped her husband's new company launch successful dealings while Harold took the credit. When Ying-ying came to visit their new house in Woodside, Lena finally had to face reality and reconsider her life and marriage.

On the dedication page of *The Joy Luck Club*, Amy Tan wrote: "To my mother and the memory of her mother. You asked me once what I would remember. This, and much more." The act of writing *The Joy Luck Club* was a journey for Tan to understand her mother Daisy as well as the strained relationship between them. Jing-mei's narrative that opens the story sets the tone for the whole book. Jing-mei recalls that her mother has told her the same story about the past multiple times over the years, "except for the ending, which grew darker, casting long shadows into her life, and eventually into mine" (*Club,* 7). While Jing-mei was growing up, her mother's stories about China were no more than fairy tales to her. She rarely considered them relevant to her life. She was, after all, an American. Other daughter characters in the novel share this belief. As Lena says, when her mother speaks to her in Chinese she "could understand the words perfectly, but not the meanings" (*Club,* 109). In the stories of the four families, the cultural differences between the mothers and daughters are literal as well as symbolic. They speak different languages: Chinese for the mothers and "perfect American" English for the daughters.

All the mothers wanted their children to "have the best combination: American circumstances and Chinese character," but they did not realize "these two things do not mix" (*Club,* 289). While the mothers made efforts to preserve their Chinese roots, the daughters strived to assimilate as much as possible during their childhood and young adulthood. Each of them had her fair share of struggles with identity and parental expectations. In the end, each character realized the similarities shared by the mothers and daughters: "[t]he same happiness, the same sadness, the same good fortune, the same faults" (*Club,* 292). Tan's "complex portrayals of mother-daughter relationships reveal the depth of familial bonds as well as intricate cultural and generational differences" (Dong b, 1205). All the mothers wanted the best for their daughters while all the daughters thought they could shun their Chinese heritage as well as the influences from their mothers. It took time for all the characters to understand one another's hopes and love.

DISCUSSION QUESTIONS

- What do the four pairs of mothers and daughters share in common? What makes each pair distinguishable from the others?
- *The Joy Luck Club* is full of cultural symbols and metaphors; for example, mah jong and the swan feather, among others. Refer to a few specific examples and discuss their meanings and functions in the book.
- Even though *The Joy Luck Club* features mainly Chinese and Chinese American characters, it reflects important themes that apply to many readers regardless of their cultural background. Discuss the universal themes in the novel.
- Discuss the unique structure of *The Joy Luck Club* that includes sixteen interwoven stories in four sections. How does such an organization help the storytelling flow? What are the connections between the sixteen stories?
- Suyuan Woo is the only character whose story is narrated through her daughter Jing-mei (June) in the book. What is the importance of her absence and how does it affect the plot, character, and structure of the book?
- Try the fourteen-question quiz on *The Joy Luck Club* online at CliffsNotes: http://www.cliffsnotes.com/WileyCDA/LitNote/id-39,pageNum-39.html.
- Try the twenty-five-question quiz on *The Joy Luck Club* online at SparkNotes: http://www.sparknotes.com/lit/joyluck/quiz.html.

4

THE KITCHEN GOD'S WIFE
(1991)

After a period of struggle to overcome the "angst of the second book," Amy Tan proved her literary talent once again by presenting to readers and critics an equally successful novel, *The Kitchen God's Wife*. It reached the *New York Times* best sellers list within a month after its publication by G. P. Putnam's Sons in 1991 and remained there for thirty-eight weeks. Later this book was included on similar best sellers lists in Australia, Canada, Denmark, England, Germany, Norway, and Spain (Snodgrass, 18–19) and overall was well accepted internationally. It won the *Booklist* Editor's Choice Award and nomination for the Bay Area Book Reviewers citation. Often compared to works by renowned authors Fyodor Dostoevsky, Boris Pasternak, and Leo Tolstoy, Tan's second novel appealed to readers of different backgrounds (Snodgrass, 18). Printed on the back cover of the Ivy Books paperback edition, the *New York Times* book review praises the book as "remarkable ... mesmerizing ... compelling.... An entire world unfolds in a Tolstoyan tide of event and detail." Page numbers cited from *The Kitchen God's Wife* in this chapter are from the 1991 paperback edition (New York: Ballantine Books, a division of Random House).

Plot Summary

The Kitchen God's Wife begins with "The Shop of the Gods," a chapter narrated by Pearl Louie Brandt. Pearl introduces a number of characters to the reader through memories of the past and present-day family gatherings, including Grand Auntie Du Ching's funeral after she died unexpectedly of a concussion caused by a traffic accident at the age of ninety-seven, and Pearl's cousin Bao-bao (Roger) Kwong's fourth engagement party at the Water Dragon Restaurant. The Louie family includes Pearl's father Jimmy, an American-born Chinese who passed away years ago; her mother Winnie (maiden name Jiang Weili) who was born and raised in China and immigrated to the United States as an adult; Pearl, married with two children; and her younger brother Samuel who lives in New Jersey when the novel begins. The Kwong family includes Uncle Henry (Kuang An) and Aunt Helen (Hulan), both of whom are immigrants from China, and their American-born children Mary, Frank, and Bao-Bao. Winnie and Helen are not sisters by blood or marriage. But they have known each other for so long that the two families became relatives and their children became cousins. In the opening chapter, Pearl sets the stage for the plot development in the rest of the book by revealing that she has been diagnosed with multiple sclerosis. Her relationship with her husband, Phil, has become uncomfortable because of it, and worst of all, she cannot bring herself to tell her mother about the terrible disease. Since it has been years since the initial diagnosis, coupled with the fact that Auntie Helen and her daughter Mary already know, telling her mother seems to be an impossible mission that haunts Pearl. Through Pearl's recollection, the reader is informed that her father Jimmy Louie died of stomach cancer when she was fourteen. Denying the loss, Pearl could not cry or mourn her father when he passed away; she ran away from the parlor and missed the funeral.

Grand Auntie Du Ching was Helen's aunt but was quite close to Winnie. It was Winnie who took care of Grand Auntie Du during her last years. When Grand Auntie Du leaves Pearl an altar to the Kitchen God, it is Winnie who tells the story of the Kitchen God and his wife to Pearl and her family. Once upon a time, a farmer named Zhang was blessed with abundance and a good wife named Guo. Later Zhang fooled around with a young woman, Lady Li, a careless squanderer who chased away the good wife. The spendthrift couple wasted money quickly. When Zhang lost all his wealth, Li left him. Now a poor and starving beggar, Zhang was waiting to die on the road when a woman saved him and took him in. Upon finding out from the maid that the kindhearted lady was his good wife Guo, Zhang was too ashamed to face her. He hastily jumped into the fireplace in the kitchen when she walked into the house. Since he recognized his mistake, the Jade Emperor made Zhang the Kitchen God who supervises other people and reports to heaven once a year. Not very important in the hierarchy of Chinese deities, the Kitchen God was nonetheless revered and worshipped by many. People would offer him tea, oranges, and other objects to show respect in the hope that he would bring good luck to them in the following year.

The novel has a structure of a story within a story; that is, Winnie's story is framed within Pearl's narrative. After the first two chapters told in Pearl's voice, the book switches to a first-person narrative by Winnie. Named Jiang Weili at birth, Winnie was born into a wealthy family in Shanghai. However, her childhood was not filled with love and joy. Winnie's mother, the second wife of a rich man, disappeared when she was only six years old. She never found out what really happened but had to endure various rumors, the disgrace her mother brought to the family, and the lack of parental care and love. Winnie grew up in her uncle's house on an island outside Shanghai with enough clothes, food, and support for education, but without love. After her arranged marriage to Wen Fu, an evil man, her life went downhill. Winnie's voice reveals her personal story side by side with the war in China. Her saga depicts her inner struggle to keep on living with Wen Fu, her incurable pain at losing her young children one after another, and her friendship with other women including Helen. She had to endure hardships caused by the mysterious disappearance of her mother, the abandonment of her father, an unfaithful and abusive husband, and the war from the 1930s to the 1940s. Winnie's narrative also brings the reader to multiple locations as she travels across China from the east to the southwest to escape the invading Japanese troops, in the process revealing the terror of war. The complexity of characters, themes, and plot makes the reading experience an emotional journey.

Winnie's narrative ends with the secret she has been afraid to tell Pearl for decades because that is the part she always wanted to forget. After receiving Jimmy's telegram telling her to come to the United States immediately, Winnie cashed in her gold and some of her jewelry on the black market in order to get a visa and tickets to get out of Shanghai. Right before her departure, Wen Fu stalked her, raped her, and almost took away her tickets and visa. Winnie left China by plane five days before the Communists took over Shanghai. Nine months later she had a baby girl, Pearl.

Winnie's story, told in twenty-one chapters, forms most of the novel until the very end when Pearl's voice returns in the second to last chapter, "Bao-Bao's Wedding." After Winnie ends her narrative by matter-of-factly saying that nine months after being raped by Wen Fu she had a baby girl, Pearl almost falls off her chair. She finally understands her mother who has been keeping such a secret from everybody and decides to reveal her own secret—her multiple sclerosis. Eventually Pearl is able to see what is left in her mother's heart: hope. After a single mother-daughter conversation that covers a time span of more than half a century, Winnie and Pearl appear in harmony at Bao-Bao's wedding ceremony. Winnie's voice narrates the very last chapter, "Sorrowfree," and closes the novel with a happy ending. She purchases a nameless goddess statue, a factory mistake, paints the name "Lady Sorrowfree" on the bottom, and gives it to Pearl with the hope that it will bring joy, luck, and much more to her daughter.

CHARACTERS, THEMES, AND SETTINGS

With a mother telling the story of her past to her daughter, *The Kitchen God's Wife* is another riveting narrative about memory and inheritance. Amy Tan's second novel further confirms her talent as a storyteller who can transcend the past, present, and future. Directly inspired by her mother Daisy's life experience, especially her disastrous first marriage and her life during wartime in China, Tan presents another touching novel set in multiple locations in China and the United States. The novel begins with Pearl's narrative set in San Jose where she lives with her husband and children, and in San Francisco where she grew up and her mother Winnie now lives. Pearl and her husband, Phil Brandt, have two daughters, eight-year-old Tessa and three-year-old Cleo. At the beginning of the story Pearl has recently accepted a position as a speech and language clinician with the local school district. Pearl and Phil's seemingly smooth life after she was diagnosed with multiple sclerosis has made Pearl uncomfortable. They used to have big arguments and disagreements. Perhaps out of fear of the unpredictable, they have stopped talking about the future and strive to lead a "normal" life in the here and now. Pearl has been hiding the diagnosis from her mother of a disease that can only be described in medical texts as "without known etiology," "extremely variable," "unpredictable," and "without specific treatment" (*Wife,* 24). Even her husband, a medical professional, cannot find adequate information about it.

Growing up, Pearl and her mother Winnie did not get along well. As an adult, Pearl confesses that Winnie's various hypotheses, in which "religion, medicine, and superstitions all merge with her own beliefs," always annoy her (*Wife,* 27). Her father Jimmy's sudden death further distanced Winnie and Pearl. It is through an unusual conversation between mother and daughter that Pearl finds out about Winnie's life in China. After both of them reveal their respective secrets, they find understanding and love.

Born into a rich family in Shanghai, Weili (Winnie) did not enjoy a happy childhood. Weili's mother, an educated beauty, was the only child

Amy Tan begins her essay "Angst and the Second Book" by saying that "I am glad that I shall never again have to write a Second Book" (*The Opposite Fate,* 324). As Tan heard repeatedly from other writers and friends, a writer's second book is doomed to fail, especially if the first is a great success. Given the fact that her debut novel, *The Joy Luck Club,* was unexpectedly and overwhelmingly well accepted, Tan had double the difficulty in breaking through her angst to write her second book. Carrying such a weight through the writing process, Tan told the reader that she "had to fight for every single character, every image, every word" (*Fate,* 333); had to write and rewrite multiple stories; and had to throw away roughly a thousand pages before moving on to complete *The Kitchen God's Wife.*

Keeping her mother in mind as the imagined reader the way she did with her first book, Tan wrote her second novel in a smooth language style that flows well and captures the characters' touching stories in a unique way. The narrative creates and unfolds family and personal secrets so seamlessly that many readers have found it hard to put the book down before finishing it. Tan considers *The Kitchen God's Wife* her favorite book (Snodgrass, 19).

of a Ningbo father and a Soochow mother. She became the second wife of Jiang Sao-Yen, a longtime friend of her late father's. As Weili remembers it, her loving mother disappeared when she was six. Shortly after that, her father sent Weili to live with his younger brother on Tsungming Island. The mysterious situation of her mother's disappearance and the later gossip created confusion and disgrace for young Weili. In her uncle's house, Weili spent years with her uncle's wives, Old Aunt and New Aunt, her cousin Huazheng (nicknamed Peanut), and a number of male cousins. Not being loved and embraced, Weili always felt like a guest. In her uncle's house, Weili acquired skills in housekeeping, cooking, and sewing that turned out to be useful for her future life. She later went to a Christian boarding school in Shanghai and she never saw her father until shortly before her marriage.

At the age of nineteen, Weili married Wen Fu as arranged by her in-laws, Old Aunt, New Aunt, her father, and the matchmaker. Right after their wedding, Wen Fu underwent training at the American Air Force School in the spring of 1937 in Hangchow, where Weili met Hulan, wife of a vice-captain pilot, Long Jiaguo. However, their peaceful life did not last long. When Japanese invaded Shanghai, the pilots under training flew out to fight and suffered heavy losses. Soon after that, the wives were sent to

Yangchow to live in a rundown house, waiting for their husbands to return. During the intervals between battles, Weili would treat Wen Fu and his fellow pilots with culinary delicacies purchased with her dowry money. When winter came, Weili and the other wives moved to Nanking with the Air Force once again. In Nanking, Weili encountered Japanese troops for the first time: an air raid took place when Weili was shopping in the marketplace with Hulan. She was six months pregnant at the time. They left Nanking that day with one suitcase for each person and only one hour to pack, sailed on the Yangtze River to Hanko-Wuchang, and then fled to Kunming by truck. It was a long and bumpy journey. Later Weili found out that she was lucky to escape the ferocious Rape of Nanking. What makes the atrocity of war more heartbreaking is Weili's statement to her daughter: "I was not affected. I was not killed" (*Wife*, 295). Together with a truckload of people, Weili traveled past Changsha, Kweiyang, and a number of towns and villages before arriving at Kunming. In the midst of the hardships caused by the war, Weili had her first baby, a stillborn girl who never cried or took one breath of air. She named her Mochou (meaning "sorrow free") after a lake in Nanking.

At the beginning of 1939, Weili had her second child, another girl. She named her Yiku (meaning "pleasure over bitterness"), hoping that in her daughter's life comfort and pleasure would cancel out hardship. Wen Fu was such an evil man that little Yiku at the age of six months learned to stop crying and curled up in a small ball the minute her father walked into the room. She became a strange baby who would not look at people's faces and would repeat her father's curses. In the summer of 1940, Weili was six months pregnant with her third baby when she had to watch helplessly as seventeen-month-old Yiku died from diarrhea while Wen Fu played mah jong with the doctor and some others. A few months later, Danru (meaning "nonchalance") was born, a boy resembling Wen Fu in appearance. Weili told herself not to love the baby so that it would not be too painful if she had to lose him. Weili left the hospital and arrived home with the milk nurse, only to find a young woman sleeping in her bed and wearing one of her nightgowns.

It was on that day Weili met Grand Auntie Du Ching, Hulan's aunt who traveled a long way from her hometown by train, boat, truck, and foot. Weili let the young woman, Min, stay in her house and become Wen Fu's mistress whom he later chased away. During wartime, Weili had a number of abortions since there was no birth control then and she did not want to bring another child into this miserable world. Even though Weili had attempted to leave Wen Fu more than once, she had to give up for fear of losing custody of her son Danru. In the summer of 1941, Japanese airplanes started to bomb Kungming; Weili and Hulan, together with Danru and Grand Auntie Du, had to evacuate the city frequently. During Christmastime of 1941, Weili attended her first dance party at the American Club where she fell in love at first sight with Jimmy Louie, a charming and handsome American-born Chinese man working for the United States Information Service. It was Jimmy who gave Wen Fu, Weili, Jiaguo, and Hulan their American names: Judas, Winnie, Jack, and Helen respectively.

By the time the war was over in the summer of 1945, Weili had been stuck in her marriage for eight years and in Kunming for seven years. Together with Jiaguo, Hulan, and Grand Auntie Du, Weili and Wen Fu left Kunming by bus with many suitcases and boxes. On their long journey back to Shanghai, Weili witnessed the dreadful aftermath of the war and the appalling damage to property as well as to people. Even worse, the end of the world war did not stop the fighting between the Kuomintang and the Communists; the civil war escalated. In Wuchang, Weili and Hulan parted ways: Hulan and Grand Auntie Du followed Jiaguo north to his new post in Harbin while Wen Fu, Weili, and Danru went east to Nanking by train and then to Shanghai by boat. Their homecoming to the Jiangs' house was different from what they had expected. During the war, Weili's father, Jiang Sao-Yen, was coaxed into collaborating with the Japanese, suffered a severe stroke, and was considered a traitor by the Kuomintang after the war ended.

The character of Wen Fu is portrayed as the representation of evil: an unfaithful husband, an abusive father, and a monstrous and greedy man. Weili first met Wen Fu when she was eighteen. At the time, Wen Fu was flirting with her cousin Huazheng. When he found out Weili's father was a wealthy merchant in Shanghai, he proposed to Weili instead. At the beginning, Weili considered him a charming, funny, and daring man but realized his evil nature as time went by. Wen Fu's life was filled with lies. He joined the Air Force by using his deceased brother's name, Wen Chen, who had graduated with top honors from a merchant seaman school. While many of his fellow pilots died fighting against the invading Japanese, he always turned his plane around to avoid confrontation and thus saved his life. During their stay in Kunming, Wen Fu took a girl for a ride in an Air Force jeep without authorization and killed her in a severe accident. After this disastrous crash, Wen Fu became worse. He drank heavily while Weili supported the family's everyday life by using her dowry money; he abused his wife and baby daughter frequently; and he raped the fourteen-year-old servant girl while his wife was in the hospital delivery room. The servant girl died from an abortion after Weili sent her away with three months' wages, a good recommendation, and the hope that she would find a better place to work.

In 1946, Weili brought Danru to Tsungming Island to visit Uncle, Old Aunt, and New Aunt. Through her aunts, Weili found out that her cousin Huazheng had run away from her in-laws' home, was divorced, and had joined the Communists. After returning to Shanghai, Weili started searching for Huazheng and in the process ran into Jimmy on the street. Five years after their first meeting, they were still attracted to each other. Weili finally made up her mind and ran away from Wen Fu. She and Danru first stayed with Huazheng and some other women for a month and then moved to Jimmy's apartment. The three of them spent some happy time together, but Weili could not get a divorce. To protect Danru from Wen Fu's vengeful searching, Weili and Jimmy sent him to Harbin to live with Hulan and Jiaguo. Danru and Jiaguo, however, died from a fast-moving epidemic later.

In 1947, Weili was arrested when she walked out of a beauty parlor. She was charged with stealing her husband's son and letting him die, for stealing valuables from her husband's family, and for deserting her husband and having an affair with an American soldier. Based on Wen Fu's lies and false charges, the judge sentenced Weili to two years in jail. Wen Fu also used the local newspaper to create a scandal and force Jimmy to leave Shanghai. Heartbroken and jobless, Jimmy boarded the *SS Marine Lynx* to the United States, determined to wait for his reunion with Weili.

After his arrival in San Francisco, Jimmy sent letters and money to Grand Auntie Du regularly so that she could stay in Shanghai and help Weili. While Weili served her time in jail, Hulan was married again to Kuang An (Henry) Kwong. Thanks to Grand Auntie Du's help, Weili was released several months early. Upon receiving Jimmy's telegram asking her to join him in the United States as his wife, Weili left China. Jimmy became a minister of a church in San Francisco, where he and Winnie had Pearl and Samuel.

What tormented Weili was the fact that none of the fellow pilots or friends would try to help her by stopping Wen Fu during their years of marriage. Instead, they stood by and watched as he bossed around and abused her. As Weili tells the reader, she was similar to the Kitchen God's wife who nobody worshipped. The Kitchen God received all the excuses and all the credit while she was forgotten. Following the lesson she learned from Old Aunt—not to strike a flea on a tiger's head (that is to say, not to solve a small problem by causing a bigger one)—Weili decided to say nothing and do nothing. She made herself blind and deaf to Wen Fu's evil behavior. Over time, Wen Fu did not change but Weili changed little by little. She learned to pretend and cover up her true feelings. She tried hard to keep her mouth shut so that the house would be peaceful. In Weili's narrative, it was quite clear that it was always women who suffered and bore the blame, while men rarely took responsibility for their bad behavior.

Upon returning to Shanghai after the war, Wen Fu pretended to be a Kuomintang war hero and took over the Jiangs' house and let all his relatives move in. The Wens wasted money and sold the Jiangs' fine furniture one piece after another. When Weili ran away to live with Jimmy, Wen Fu hired gangsters to terrorize Weili's divorce lawyer and filed false charges against her that eventually put her in jail. At the same time he took another wife and continued to live in the Jiangs' house. Forty years after Weili escaped from Wen Fu, the mention of his name still filled her with deep fear. Years later a letter from a friend in Hong Kong tells Winnie the bad man died peacefully of a bad heart at the age of seventy-eight.

As Pearl tells the reader, the Kwongs are not relatives by blood but over the years have become extended family for the Louies. Auntie Helen and Winnie have been co-owners of the Ding Ho Flower Shop in Chinatown for twenty-five years. Mary (Helen's daughter by her second husband Henry) and Pearl are about the same age and have a strained friendship when the story opens. Their husbands went to the same medical school. Mary, Doug, and their teenaged children, Jennifer and Michael, now live in Los Angeles. To some degree, Pearl's relationship with Mary resembles that between Winnie and Helen. They have been friends for years but they always get on each other's nerves.

Tan portrays the minor characters with uniqueness and subtlety. She conveys the image of Weili's father, Jiang Sao-Yen, as stubborn and arrogant through Weili's brief encounters with him. Weili states that even though her father knew about the Wen family's bad reputation, he still accepted the marriage proposal probably because she was not considered a good daughter. In describing Weili's loneliness during girlhood and her ignorance about pregnancy as a young woman, the novel shows how Old Aunt and New Aunt failed to provide the necessary parental care and guidance. Through cousin Huazheng's escape story, the book also indicates the struggle and changing situation of Chinese women during and after the war. Overall, the novel provides a vivid collage of characters through the narratives of Weili and Pearl.

DISCUSSION QUESTIONS

• Discuss the relationship between Winnie and Helen as well as that between Pearl and Mary. To what extent does the younger generation's friendship resemble that of their mothers and to what extent is it different?

- Analyze the character of Winnie in relation to the other characters in the novel: her father Jiang Sao-Yen, her mother, her first husband Wen Fu, her second husband Jimmy Louie, and her daughter Pearl. What are her strengths and what are her weaknesses?
- Analyze the character Wen Fu in relation to the other characters in the novel: his wife Winnie, his mother Wen Tai-tai, his father-in-law Jiang Sao-Yen, and the other pilots. Do you think this character is evil? Cite specific examples to explain why or why not.
- Discuss Tan's description of wartime China in the novel through Winnie's eyes. What does her narrative tell the reader about the effect of war on Chinese people of different social classes?
- Comparing Tan's first novel, *The Joy Luck Club*, with her second, *The Kitchen God's Wife,* what are the major similarities and differences of themes and settings?
- Try the online quiz on *The Kitchen God's Wife* at SparkNotes: http://www.sparknotes.com/lit/kitchengods/quiz.html.

5

THE HUNDRED SECRET SENSES
(1995)

Dedicated to her editor and longtime friend Faith Sale, Amy Tan's third novel, *The Hundred Secret Senses*, received critical praise and was another national best seller. This work shows a departure from Tan's previously published novels in the sense that the book focuses on sisterly bonds instead of mother-daughter relationships. It reveals mesmerizing stories about the characters' previous and current lives to the point that it is difficult to distinguish the real world and the dream or spiritual world. *The Hundred Secret Senses* has been considered a "magic realistic text" (Adams 2005, 125). Tan may have incorporated some elements of her unpublished manuscript *The Year of No Flood*, a historical novel, into *The Hundred Secret Senses* (Snodgrass, 19). Page numbers cited from *The Hundred Secret Senses* in this chapter are from the 1998 paperback edition (New York: Vintage, a division of Random House).

Plot Summary

The Hundred Secret Senses begins with Olivia Yee Lagnuni Bishop's narrative about her half sister Kwan Li who believes she has *yin* eyes and therefore can see people who have passed away. Kwan insists on calling them *yin* people instead of ghosts. Olivia's voice introduces her family and other characters as well. Olivia's father, Jack Yee, was married to

Li Chen when he was a student in Guilin, China. In 1944, the couple had a daughter, Kwan. Li Chen died four years later. When Jack went to Hong Kong hoping to find a job, he left Kwan in the care of Li Chen's sister, Li Bin-bin, in Changmian, a small village near Guilin, and sent money to support them. After he immigrated to the United States in 1949, Jack married Louise Kenfield, a Caucasian, and started a new life. They had three biracial children—Kevin, Olivia, and Tommy—and raised their family in San Francisco. When Olivia was barely four years old, Jack passed away because of renal failure. Right before his death, Jack confessed to Louise about his previous marriage and his daughter, Kwan. He asked Louise to bring her over to the United States as his last wish.

Two years after Jack's death, Louise was remarried to Bob Lagnuni, an Italian American. Olivia was nearly six when Kwan finally came to the United States, a short and chubby teenager who spoke no English at all. Olivia not only had to share a bedroom with Kwan, but she also spent a lot of time with her while Louise visited beauty parlors or shopped with friends. As Olivia put it, by the first grade she became "an expert on public humiliation and shame" because Kwan asked many dumb questions (*Senses*, 11). In many ways, Kwan took care of Olivia and her brothers when they were children, filling a mother's role since Louise was so often absent. Instead of feeling grateful, young Olivia resented Kwan for taking her mother's place. Furthermore, Kwan filled Olivia's childhood with strange stories. Night after night, Olivia would fall asleep while Kwan told one story after another. When she woke up, Kwan would still be talking in Chinese. Olivia became the only one in her family who learned Chinese (involuntarily) due to Kwan's influence. Kwan's stories filled Olivia's childhood imagination with an abundance of graphic pictures about the past and Guilin and the village of Changmian in China.

Beginning in the second chapter, "Fisher of Man," Olivia begins to reveal the stories that Kwan had told her during the years in which they shared the same bedroom. Olivia's narrative about her American life is intertwined with Kwan's narrative about her own life in China, as well as a previous life more than a century ago in which both sisters were loyal friends. Kwan's story about this previous life is told in the first person and is set against the backdrop of the Taiping Rebellion (also known as the Heavenly Kingdom, 1851–1864) against the Manchu government in China.

In their previous lives, Kwan was Nunumu (also known as Miss Moo) and Olivia was Miss Nelly Banner. A Hakka (one of the ethnic minorities in China) coming from a small place on the Thistle Mountain south of Changmian, Guangxi Province, seven-year-old Nunumu lost one eye when a rock tumbled down the mountain. In 1864 when she was fourteen, by chance she met Miss Banner and the Jesus Worshippers from England and went to live with them in the Ghost Merchant's House, doing laundry, cleaning, and other household chores for the foreigners. Nunumu and Miss Banner became good friends. During her stay in the Ghost Merchant's House, Nunumu and Miss Banner had a short period of misunderstanding because of Cape, a westerner who deceived the Hakka people. He recruited them to fight for the rebellion by making false promises, claiming to be working on behalf of the Heavenly King, and then betrayed them by switching his allegiance to the Manchus. This immoral man unfortunately won the heart of Miss Banner and stayed in the Ghost Merchant's House for months as her lover. Cape disappeared suddenly one day, taking away everybody's valuables and leaving behind Miss Banner with humiliation and a broken heart. As the battles between the Manchus, aided by westerners, and the forces of the Taiping Rebellion came to the last stage, traffic between Canton and Guangxi was blocked. As a result, the Jesus Worshippers no longer received supplies and had to survive on their own. During this difficult time, Miss Banner and Yiban, the son of an American father and a Chinese mother who worked as Cape's translator, fell in love. In 1870 when Nunumu was twenty years old, the Manchu soldiers squelched the Taiping Rebellion and took over Changmian as well as other nearby regions. The Jesus Worshippers, Miss Banner, and Nunumu all died in the chaos.

In her American life, thirty-eight-year-old Olivia had been separated from her husband Simon for a few months. On the eve of getting a divorce, the couple took a trip to China for a photo essay on village cuisine for a travel magazine, *Lands Unknown*. Kwan accompanied them to visit her home. They first landed in Guilin before making their way to Changmian, Kwan's native town. A small village located between two jagged mountain peaks, Changmian had avoided modernization. In Olivia's eyes it looked like "a fabled misty land, half memory, half illusion" (*Senses*, 205). Olivia felt the landscape was at once remote and familiar upon her arrival: it was so different from her hometown, San Francisco, and so far away from her American life, yet it was the setting of Kwan's stories that she had grown up with and it had appeared in her dreams and imagination repeatedly. Their two-week stay was filled with surprises and changed everybody's life. It was during the stay in Changmian without modern conveniences, such as hot water or a refrigerator, that Olivia reflected upon her relationships with Simon and Kwan.

In the end, Olivia and Simon reconciled and surprisingly expected their first baby. Meanwhile, Kwan disappeared into the valley of caves. The closing chapter tells the reader that two years after returning to San Francisco, Olivia now lives with her fourteen-month-old daughter, Samantha, and has changed her last name to "Li," Kwan's family name from her mother. Simon visits during weekends and the three of them enjoy family time while Olivia and Simon keep working on their relationship.

CHARACTERS, THEMES, AND SETTINGS

Both born in the Year of the Monkey but twelve years apart, the half sisters Kwan and Olivia are quite different. When the book opens, Olivia is a thirty-eight-year-old commercial photographer who is struggling in the middle of a divorce with her husband and business-writing partner, Simon Bishop. Olivia lost her father at a young age and grew up with a mother who frequently changed boyfriends, occupied her days with shopping and meetings with friends, and did not have much time for her children. Kwan had been the main caregiver for Olivia since she was six. Having a photographic memory and a childhood filled with Kwan's strange stories about the *yin* people, Olivia is obsessed with her own imaginative world and dreams.

Twelve years older than Olivia, Kwan Li is almost fifty when the narrative begins. Kwan grew up in a small village with her aunt Li Bin-bin, known as Big Ma, and moved to the United States when she was a teenager due to her father's deathbed wish. Olivia notes that Kwan never fits in with her American family, does not resemble her father or any of her half siblings, and probably never will be Americanized. Although miniature at barely five feet tall, Kwan is loud and daring since her arrival in San Francisco. As Olivia tells the reader, Kwan has many unusual abilities, such as being able to pinpoint the source of faults in electronic equipment, to diagnose people's ailments, and to calm people and release their worries. A warmhearted caregiver to her half siblings, a marvelous storyteller, and a loyal friend to Olivia, Kwan is a charming character who speaks Pidgin English and has a special instinct about human relationships. Tan gives such a vivid description of Kwan that she becomes the most memorable character in the novel. A review in the *San Jose Mercury News* called Kwan "a great raconteur, a great talker, a great fictional invention" (*Senses,* fly page). The *New York Times* book review stated, "Kwan, in particular, is a memorable creation ... at once innocent and wise.... We could all do with such a sister" (*Senses,* fly page). The *Hartford Chronicle* remarked: "In Kwan, she's created a woman so vivid, you can almost see her badly permed hair, hear her raspy voice, smell the garlic on her hands" (*Senses,* fly page).

Olivia and Kwan have an interesting relationship. In Olivia's narrative, the reader can see how Kwan has adored her and taken care of her since childhood. Yet it takes years before Olivia realizes the importance of Kwan in her life and the bond between them. She resented Kwan as a child, a teenager, and even as an adult, and thus frequently felt guilty in the face of Kwan's sincere concern and love for her. Kwan's presence and her stories helped shape Olivia's childhood as well as her life as an adult. To Olivia, Kwan is a sister as well as a mother figure. In this sense, their relationship resembles the bond between immigrant mothers and American-born daughters that has appeared in Tan's earlier works.

In her current life, Olivia is struggling in her relationship with Simon, a half-Hawaiian man whom she loves but feels does not love her enough. When Olivia first met Simon in a linguistics class at the University of California at Berkeley in 1976, she thought she had found her male doppelganger, another Eurasian whose name did not fit with his Asian features. She fell in love quickly only to realize Simon still loved his girlfriend, Elza, who died in a ski accident a few months before. Because Simon and Elza had a fight right before the accident, Simon felt responsible for her sudden death and had a hard time overcoming the tragedy. In her relationship with Simon, Olivia always felt like a runner-up living in the shadow of Elza. Her insecurity led to many disagreements, misunderstandings, and fights. Their marriage faced other obstacles as well, such as financial difficulties, infertility, and the growing distance between them. As time went by, Olivia realized that they were compatible in some ways but they were not "special, not like people who truly belonged to each other." They were "partners, not soul mates, two separate people who happened to be sharing a menu and a life" (*Senses,* 125).

Olivia's relationship with Simon is echoed by Miss Nelly Banner's relationship with Yiban in Kwan's story of their previous lives when Olivia was Miss Banner and she was Nunumu. First having fallen in love with an evil person, Cape, Nelly eventually found her true love, Yiban, a translator for Cape and the son of a Chinese woman and an American trader. Yiban's mother committed suicide because her American lover decided not to take her along to America; she gave birth to him right after her death. As a young boy Yiban spent a few years in America before returning to China with his father, Johnson. When Yiban was fifteen, Johnson borrowed money from Cape and gave him Yiban as a guarantee that he would repay Cape. For the next fifteen years, Yiban belonged to Cape since his father never paid off the debt. Nelly and Yiban enjoyed a short period of happiness before the Manchu soldiers took over Changmian and slaughtered many, including the Jesus Worshippers.

The Hundred Secret Senses is set in San Francisco and Changmian, covering a long time span from 1864 to contemporary times. Nunumu and Nelly Banner's story is set amid the Taiping Rebellion in China in the nineteenth century in Changmian and nearby regions. Tan portrays the mountain village as a preindustrial community with mysterious colors and the beauty of nature. At the end of the story, when every character's life is changed, so is the fate of the village. Kwan's disappearance attracted many people to this unknown territory: search teams, archeologists, scientists, and then a large number of tourists.

Tan's third novel puts a different spin on the themes of family bonds and cultural identity by exploring new territory in the world of spirits and ghosts. Like Maxine Hong Kingston's acclaimed *The Woman Warrior*, *The Hundred Secret Senses* "weave[s] mysterious ghost stories with women's life experiences," in which "ghosts represent the haunting past and the cultural memory of the immigrant sisters and mothers, waiting to be remembered and then exorcised" (Lee, 116). For Kwan, the ghost stories are her medium to bridge the past with the present, China with America. For Olivia, exorcizing Elza's ghost in her mind is a necessary step to break through the barrier between her and Simon; understanding Kwan's ghost stories is a step to connect her cultural heritages.

Further differences from the Chinese American characters in Tan's earlier works lie in biracial as well as multiracial characters in *The Hundred Secret Senses*. In this sense, Tan's third novel casts light on the diverse relationships in Chinese American families and the cultural differences in Chinese American communities (Yu, 347). Both Olivia and Simon represent multiracial lineages in American society. As Sheng-mei Ma remarks, "the mixed-blood Bishops embody the cultural hybridization of a minority like Asian Americans" (Ma 2001, 30–31). On a more universal level, *The Hundred Secret Senses* is about love: different kinds of love. Tan has said: "I thought, 'This is a story about sisters and the

The supernatural elements and entanglement in the spiritual world in *The Hundred Secret Senses* have incurred mixed reception among critics and readers. Even though most reviewers were excited about Amy Tan's new experiment, others responded with unfavorable reviews of the book. For example, Tan's portrayal of China at its "most questionable" and her indulgence in "implausible mysticism" is criticized by Ping-chia Feng in her entry on "Amy Tan" in the *Dictionary of Literary Biography* (1996). After applauding Tan's first two novels, Feng states that this novel fails to develop the identity problems faced by her characters Olivia and Kwan.

[story] about the peculiar relationships of families,' but as I was writing I realized that the kind of love that Kwan was providing was this unconditional love that felt very comforting to me, and I thought that part of me is always looking for that" (Giles).

DISCUSSION QUESTIONS

- Tan has described sisterly relationships in her previous works; for example, the friendship between Winnie and Helen in *The Kitchen God's Wife*. What makes the sisterly bond between Olivia and Kwan different?
- Discuss the relationship between Olivia and Simon. What went wrong between them and how does their relationship change as the story progresses?
- Analyze the character of Simon Bishop, in terms of his relationships with Elza, Olivia, and Kwan.
- *The Hundred Secret Senses* has multiple story lines: Kwan's life in the Chinese village of Changmian; Olivia's childhood with Kwan as her main caregiver; Olivia's present life with Simon; Kwan and Olivia's previous lives as Nunumu and Miss Banner, among others. How does the author structure the novel to tie these stories together? How does the plot develop with intertwined story lines progressing at the same time?
- Tan has used Guilin (also spelled Kweilin) as a geographical setting in *The Joy Luck Club* and *The Kitchen God's Wife*. How is the cultural setting of Changmian, a village near Guilin, different in *The Hundred Secret Senses*?
- Olivia's struggle to communicate in Chinese during her trip to Changmian to some degree echoes Kwan's experience of learning English in San Francisco. How does the novel use language to portray cultural differences between the characters (Kwan and Olivia) and the settings (San Francisco and Changmian)?
- What does the ending of the novel mean to Olivia, to Simon, to Kwan, and to you as a reader?
- Compared to Tan's previously published works, *The Joy Luck Club* and *The Kitchen God's Wife*, what are the distinguishing features of *The Hundred Secret Senses*? What do the books share in common as novels?
- Asian American scholar Sheng-mei Ma has criticized Amy Tan's creation of "a New Age ethnicity mongrelized with primitivism, that appeals to westerners' long-held Orientalist view of Asians and Asia" (Ma 2000, xxii). Do you agree with him based on your reading of *The Hundred Secret Senses*? Why and why not?

6

THE BONESETTER'S DAUGHTER
(2001)

A few years after being diagnosed with Alzheimer's disease, Amy Tan's mother, Daisy, passed away on November 22, 1999, surrounded by loved ones. Shortly after her mother's funeral, Tan lost her editor, Faith Sale, to cancer on December 7, 1999; Faith had been a good friend and mentor for years. Suffering from both losses, the writing process of her fourth novel turned out to be difficult, but in the end Tan produced another critically appraised and best-selling work, *The Bonesetter's Daughter*. The intensity of feelings and emotions that penetrates this novel has touched many readers' hearts and won favorable comments from reviewers and scholars. As Tan told the press, *The Bonesetter's Daughter* is her most personal publication because "it traces the lives of two narrators, a mother and daughter, and their struggle to resolve their relationship" (Darraj, 91). Page numbers cited from *The Bonesetter's Daughter* in this chapter are from the 2001 paperback edition (New York: Ballantine Books, a division of Random House).

PLOT SUMMARY

The Bonesetter's Daughter includes an introduction, seventeen chapters divided into three parts, and an epilogue. The introductory chapter, "Truth," sets forth a number of important themes of the novel: family, love, secrets, the mother-daughter bond, as well as lost and recollected memories. This short narrative by LuLing Young also introduces some of her family members: her two late husbands Pan Kai Jing and Edwin Young, and her daughter Ruth Luyi Young. Then the story quickly shifts to the past as LuLing recalls one winter morning when she was six. It was the day when Precious Auntie told LuLing her family name, the name of all the bonesetters, and asked her never to forget it. Yet when the narrative opens, LuLing is struggling to remember the forgotten name, which is not disclosed until the end of the book.

Part One presents a third-person description of Ruth and LuLing's American life at present in San Francisco. The seven numbered chapters focus primarily on Ruth's life, her career, and her relationships with other characters, and reflect on her childhood in flashbacks. Part One begins with Ruth's account of how she would lose her voice for a week starting on August twelfth each year ever since she moved into her partner Art's flat. Working as a ghostwriter, Ruth is struggling in her relationship with her mother and with Art as well as searching for happiness and the real meaning of her own life. On the last day of her ninth annual week of silence, Ruth discovered a long neglected stack of paper in the bottom of a drawer: pages her mother wrote in Chinese about her family, childhood, and life experience. Ruth had put away these pages years before due to her lack of interest and very limited reading skills in the Chinese language.

Ruth's interest in her mother's writing was rekindled when LuLing was diagnosed with Alzheimer's disease. After sending her mother to spend a few days with her aunt GaoLing, Ruth went to clean her mother's apartment that was cluttered with rancid food, junk mail, and other paraphernalia. Seeing many of the familiar objects reminded Ruth of her childhood and her conflicts with LuLing during her teenage years. It was during this process of remembering the past and reconsidering her own life that Ruth decided "she would ask her mother to tell her about her life. For once, she would ask. She would listen. She would sit down and not be in a hurry or have anything else to do. She would even move in with her mother, spend more time getting to know her" (*Daughter,* 168). For the first time in her life, Ruth "wanted to be here, as her mother told her about her life, taking her through all the detours of the past, explaining the multiple meanings of Chinese words, how to translate her heart" (*Daughter,* 168–69). Ruth found a translator to help her understand LuLing's writing that would reveal tragedy, love, and family secrets.

In Part Two, the narrative voice becomes LuLing's, presented through her writing that Ruth is trying to decipher. The seven chapters, titled in both English words and Chinese characters ("Heart," "Change,"

"Ghost," "Destiny," "Effortless," "Character," and "Fragrance"), recount LuLing's childhood and family in China and the life of Precious Auntie. It begins with the first nineteen years of LuLing's life with the Liu clan in the village of Immortal Heart in the Western Hills south of Peking. Nicknamed Forty-six Kilometers from Reed Moat Bridge, Immortal Heart was a village with nearly two thousand residents when LuLing was growing up. The Liu clan had lived in the village for six centuries and the family house on Pig's Head Lane had grown from a simple three-pillar house to a compound with many wings and additions that were built over the years by different generations. Behind their family compound was a cliff overlooking a ravine. Known as the End of the World, the ravine was a revered and forbidden place filled with unwanted babies, suicide maidens, and beggar ghosts. The Lius were ink makers. Around 1920, male members of the family started to sell their ink in Peking and lived in the back room of a shop in the old Pottery-Glazing District for extended periods of time. As far as LuLing could remember, in the Liu family it was the women who made the ink. The novel portrays the painstaking process of ink-making in great detail.

Precious Auntie had been LuLing's nursemaid since her birth and had taken care of her on a daily basis. LuLing believed that Liu Jin Sen, the eldest son, was her father and his wife her mother. Yet in reality LuLing was the daughter of Precious Auntie and Liu Hu Sen (also known as Baby Uncle since he was the youngest and favorite son of the Liu family), who unfortunately died on his wedding day. LuLing didn't find out the truth about her biological mother until Precious Auntie passed away and left behind many sheets of paper, telling her daughter what had happened. Only when LuLing read the pages was Precious Auntie's tragic life story revealed. Precious Auntie was born in a larger town, named Zhou's Mouth of the Mountain in honor of Emperor Zhou of the Shang Dynasty, about ten kilometers from Immortal Heart. Her family had been bonesetters for nine hundred years, passing on their family heritage generation after generation. Their family had a secret location called the Monkey's Jaw for finding the best dragon bones to make medicine. Her father was the Famous Bonesetter. When Precious Auntie was four, her mother and older brothers died of an intestine-draining disease. Grief-stricken, her father spent his life savings on the funerals and spoiled his only daughter while raising her single-handedly. Because she was educated and worked as a medical assistant to her father, the Bonesetter, few sought her hand in marriage when she was of marital age.

When Precious Auntie was nineteen, two marriage proposals came to the Bonesetter: one from the coffin maker Chang and the other from Baby Uncle. Precious Auntie declined the former and accepted the latter, which infuriated the other suitor Chang. A month before the wedding, Baby Uncle came to her room late at night and the young couple consummated their nuptials early. Humiliated and angered, Chang sabotaged Precious Auntie's wedding, stole her dowry of opium and dragon bones, and was responsible for the death of her father and Baby Uncle. Becoming an orphan and a widow on her wedding day, Precious Auntie attempted to kill herself by fire in the Lius' house, but was saved by Great-Granny. Precious Auntie survived with a heavily scarred face and could not speak any more. After she gave birth to LuLing, the Lius decided to let her stay as a nursemaid and asked the eldest brother and sister-in-law to be LuLing's parents.

Growing up, LuLing was very close to Precious Auntie until she turned fourteen in 1929. It was the time when scientists came to Dragon Bone Hill at the Mouth of the Mountain searching for more bones of human ancestors after the million-year-old skullcap of the "Peking Man" was discovered. Rumors went around and all the villagers had a "fever," searching for human relics in the hope of becoming rich overnight. The coffin maker Chang became famous because some of his dragon bones turned out to be human. In order to find out the Bonesetter family's secret location, Chang proposed that LuLing marry his fourth son, Chang Fu Nan, with the secret hope that he might satisfy his greed by finding more dragon bones at the Monkey Jaw. The Liu family's happy acceptance of this proposal and LuLing's eagerness to marry into the Chang household devastated Precious Auntie. After failing to dissuade LuLing, she took her own life in order to protect her daughter because the villagers were afraid of an avenging ghost. After she killed herself in the Lius' ink studio, Precious Auntie's body was thrown into the End of the World. Upon finding out the truth of her birth parents, LuLing, heartbroken, looked for her down in the ravine but to no avail.

After the Chang family cancelled the marriage proposal out of fear of Precious Auntie's ghost, LuLing was sent to an orphanage run by American Christian missionaries at an abandoned monastery near Dragon Bone Hill. Because Precious Auntie had tutored her, she became a teacher for the younger orphans. During her stay, LuLing fell in love with Pan Kai Jing, one of the geologists unearthing the bones. A few months after the Japanese troops invaded Wanping in 1937, they were married in winter in two kinds of weddings: American and Chinese. For a short while, LuLing enjoyed a happy life with her husband, her father-in-law, and those living in the orphanage until Pan Kai Jing was taken away by the Communist soldiers for two months, and then captured and executed by the Japanese. After the war was over, LuLing's cousin GaoLing went to San Francisco with the help of the missionaries while

LuLing went to Hong Kong, taking odd jobs to support herself while waiting for a sponsorship to the United States. After staying in Hong Kong for nearly two years, LuLing finally sailed to San Francisco on a visitor's visa.

Part Three switches back to the third person, telling the reader about Ruth and LuLing's American life at the moment. After eighty-year-old Mr. Tang translated LuLing's writing into English, Ruth came to understand her mother and her family heritage. At the end of the novel, LuLing happily moved to an assisted living facility, Ruth and Art reconciled their relationship, and Ruth found out Precious Auntie's real name: Gu Liu Xin. After much contemplation, Ruth put aside her ghostwriting profession and started to write her own book, telling the stories of her grandmother, her mother, and herself.

CHARACTERS, THEMES, AND SETTINGS

The *Toronto Globe and Mail* praised Tan's fourth novel as "a riveting, multi-layered tale.... Tan's storytelling skills are strong, and her plot line appeals to the rebellious daughter in all of us" (*Daughter*, fly page). The two pairs of mothers and daughters in three generations and their complex relationships make *The Bonesetter's Daughter* rich in character and storytelling as well as touching in emotion and feeling. The reviewer for *US Weekly* extolled Tan's novel as a "suspenseful family saga set in contemporary San Francisco and in a quaint Chinese village a few decades earlier.... In agile, lyrical prose, Tan effortlessly combines the mundane and the mythical to create another dynamic multigenerational odyssey" (*Daughter*, fly page). The writings of the two mother figures reveal the family history and secrets while providing a vivid portrayal of the village Immortal Heart and the historical setting of early twentieth-century China. The story-within-a-story narrative not only helps build up each character and develop the plot, but also reflects such important historical events from the 1920s to the 1940s as the archeological discovery of Peking Man, the Japanese invasion, and the civil war between Kuomintang and the Communists in China.

One of the main characters is the daughter of the Famous Bonesetter from the Mouth of the Mountain, Precious Auntie (Bao Bomu), who is first introduced as LuLing's nursemaid. As the plot develops, the novel reveals that Precious Auntie was actually LuLing's birth mother who has suffered deeply. Her real name, Gu Liu Xin, is not disclosed until the end of the book. Precious Auntie gave LuLing the nickname Doggie. Since she had no voice, Precious Auntie raised LuLing with the soundless and strong "hand-talk, face-talk, and chalk-talk" (*Daughter*, 2). In the Liu household, LuLing was the only one who could understand her particular "language." The novel portrays the character Precious Auntie first through LuLing's childhood memory: "a sweet-peach forehead, wide-set eyes, full cheeks tapering to a small plump nose" plus a puzzle-like mouth. "Half was bumpy, half was smooth and melted closed. The inside of her right cheek was stiff as leather, the left was moist and soft. Where the gums had burned, the teeth had fallen out. And her tongue was like a parched root. She could not taste the pleasures of life: salty and bitter, sour and sharp, spicy, sweet, and fat" (*Daughter*, 3). The novel later depicts Precious Auntie's family, girlhood, and her unfortunate wedding day on which her beautiful face as well as her life was destroyed. LuLing understandably became the main hope for Precious Auntie and the only reason she would endure misery, stay in this world, and live with the Liu clan.

Having been close to Precious Auntie growing up, LuLing turned against her when she received a marriage proposal from the coffin maker Chang. LuLing was not aware of Chang's evil actions that had caused the death of her grandfather and her birth father; nor did she know about Chang's greedy motivation behind the marriage proposal. LuLing dreamed about marrying into a decent family that had recently become famous because of the bones related to the discovery of Peking Man. The conflict between Precious Auntie and LuLing only ended after Precious Auntie killed herself trying to protect her daughter who finally gains understanding by reading her mother's writing.

Years later, LuLing would immigrate to the United States and marry Edwin Young, a medical student, after living in war-torn China and Hong Kong. After Edwin died in a hit-and-run car accident, LuLing had to raise their daughter Ruth single-handedly. LuLing is portrayed as a strong-willed character in the novel. In Ruth's memory, her mother is constantly

On the dedication page of her fourth novel, Amy Tan wrote: "On the last day that my mother spent on earth, I learned her real name, as well as that of my grandmother. This book is dedicated to them." Tan's mother, Daisy, was diagnosed with Alzheimer's disease in the mid-1990s. During her last years, Daisy lost a lot of her memory and for the first time ever she became a happy person. It is ironic that Daisy finally found happiness and peace when she suffered from memory loss. Only hours before her mother's death in 1999, Amy learned her mother's real name, Li Bingzi, from her half sister.

unhappy about everything and everybody. Four feet eleven inches tall and eighty-five pounds, LuLing speaks English with a strange British accent that she acquired in Hong Kong. As far as Ruth can remember, her mother was never sick. At the age of seventy-seven, LuLing has none of the health problems common to older people. Recently, however, LuLing has become more and more forgetful, which concerns Ruth. After several tests, LuLing is diagnosed with Alzheimer's disease. After failed attempts to hire housekeepers to keep an eye on her mother and help with her daily routines, Ruth decides to take care of LuLing herself.

Ruth was born in a Water Dragon Year and LuLing in a Fire Dragon Year. Therefore they are "the same but for opposite reasons" (*Daughter*, 1). Ruth, soon to be forty-six, is a book doctor (also known as a ghost-writer) after working in corporate communications and freelance editing. Nearly fifteen years into her business, she had about thirty-five books to her credit, but whenever a book was published, Ruth had to sit back and accept the lack of acknowledgement of her work. Both in her personal life and in her work, Ruth is very accommodating and usually tries to make things easy for others. Since the age of ten, Ruth has become the translator and collaborator for her mother in dealing with the Telephone Company, banks, and other business matters. Ruth met Art, a linguist working at the Center on Deafness at the University of California at San Francisco, in an evening yoga class. Since Art's divorce, his daughters Sofia (fifteen and petite) and Dory (thirteen and chunky) had been alternating between staying with their mother Miriam, stepfather Stephen, and two half brothers Andy and Beauregard in Sausalito and with Art and Ruth on Vallejo Street.

The charm of *The Bonesetter's Daughter* lies in its touching exploration of the universal themes of family and love. The *Anniston Star* review commended the book as an "enchanting story of a mother and daughter, the secrets they have kept from one another, and the common ground they finally come to occupy…. A powerful, luminously written saga in which past and present are bound together into the tangled skein of a human life" (*Daughter*, fly page).

DISCUSSION QUESTIONS

• Discuss the role of memory in LuLing and Ruth's life. How does memory of the past affect LuLing and Ruth's present lives as well as their personalities?

- How does *The Bonesetter's Daughter* convey the characters' beliefs and the notion of destiny? Do you think Precious Auntie, LuLing, and Ruth are superstitious? Why or why not?
- Discuss the family curse that is unveiled gradually in the novel. How does it affect the characters of different generations: Precious Auntie, LuLing, and Ruth? By the end of the story, is the problem solved?
- What are the similarities as well as conflicts between the mother Precious Auntie and the daughter LuLing, and those between the mother LuLing and the daughter Ruth, despite Ruth's deliberate effort to shun her Chinese heritage and to assimilate completely?
- How does Amy Tan structure her book in a way that bridges the past to the present and provides more than one vantage point? How does Tan effectively organize the complexities in the characters' families as well as their personal histories?
- How does the novel portray the sisterly relationship between LuLing and GaoLing? What characteristics of GaoLing make her adjustment to American life different from that of LuLing? How does their relationship evolve as the story progresses?
- A family dinner in a Chinese restaurant is a recurring element in Amy Tan's novels: weddings, Chinese holidays, and other special occasions. What role does the Full Moon Festival family reunion at the Fountain Court restaurant play in *The Bonesetter's Daughter*? What does it mean to Ruth? What does it tell the reader about Ruth's life in the past and her relationships with other characters whom she considered "family" and invited to the dinner? How does it affect Ruth's life afterward?
- How is Ruth's American life (i.e., her relationship with Art, her profession as a ghostwriter, etc.) intertwined with LuLing's narrative about the past? What are the intricate connections between Ruth's reality and the history of Precious Auntie, LuLing, and their family? How does the revelation of the truth regarding the past affect Ruth's life at present?
- To what extent do the stories of Precious Auntie, LuLing, and Ruth reflect the author's personal experiences and her relationship with her mother, Daisy?

7

SAVING FISH FROM DROWNING
(2005)

Amy Tan's fifth novel, *Saving Fish from Drowning*, was a dramatic change in terms of themes, characters, and setting compared to her previous fictional works. The story no longer focuses on Chinese American characters and the setting is now Burma. In terms of book sales, *Saving Fish from Drowning* was another success story in Tan's publication history. It had been on the paperback best sellers list of *Publishers Weekly* for nine weeks by December 4, 2006. Her book tour in November 2006 enjoyed huge turnouts. Examples of positive reviews included: "*Saving Fish from Drowning* is replete with the riches that have made Tan's reputation" (*Boston Globe*), "Amy Tan's best book to date ... ingenious, funny touching" (*Sunday Telegraphy*), and "The novel has all the ingredients for a pulse-racing read ... highly entertaining" (*Guardian*; all three cited at http://amytan.net). Page numbers cited from *Saving Fish from Drowning* in this chapter are from the 2005 hardcover edition (New York: G. P. Putnam's Sons).

PLOT SUMMARY

Saving Fish from Drowning begins with "a note to the reader," in which Tan uses a fictional prologue to set off the story. She explains her accidental visit to the American Society for Psychical Research in

Manhattan, New York, where she found Bibi Chen's posthumously dictated tale. A socialite and owner of an Asian antique shop, Bibi Chen was a well-known figure in Tan's hometown of San Francisco. After her death, Bibi Chen was said to deliver her story through fifty-four automatic writing sessions with a medium named Karen Lundegaard, who lived in Berkeley, California. After several meetings with Lundegaard, careful study of Bibi Chen's story regarding the eleven American tourists missing in Mandalay, Burma, that was delivered through Lundegaard in writing, interviews with other people, and extensive research about Burma through secondary sources, the author presents this story to the reader.

The novel, divided into eighteen chapters, is told by Bibi Chen, a wealthy socialite, proprietor, and generous patron of the arts. Tan unfolds the story beginning with Bibi Chen's unexpected and mysterious death. Bibi had planned to lead a group of her friends on an art expedition to China and Burma, called "Following the Buddha's Footsteps." But at the age of sixty-three, she died under strange circumstances in her San Francisco oriental artifacts shop called "The Immortals" two weeks before the planned departure date. Partly to pay tribute to Bibi and partly because they could not get a refund of their deposits, her friends decided to carry out the Burma Road trip and selected a new group leader. Making changes to Bibi's original itinerary along the way, this group of twelve tourists first went to China and then Burma, facing one adventure after another, some of them unexpected and unpleasant. Bibi joined them as an all-seeing spirit, explaining and commenting on the events along the way. Bibi's narrative voice leads the reader through her own funeral and the failed police investigation of her sudden death before narrating the adventure of the tourists in China and Burma.

Interwoven with the tourists' trip is Bibi's reflection on her childhood and family history that has filled her with sadness. Being born to a concubine and losing her mother as an infant, Bibi was raised by her father's first wife, Sweet Ma. Unfortunately they resented each other. Even though her family in Shanghai was wealthy, Bibi grew up without much parental love and guidance. Her experience partially molds her personality into someone deficient in great feelings and always holding a blank face and blank heart. When Bibi was thirteen, her family fled Shanghai to the United States right before the Communists took over the city. By the time of Bibi's funeral, the only survivor in her family was Sweet Ma who lived in a nursing home.

When the twelve tourists entered Burma via China, Bibi was with them in the form of a spirit that can see through people's actions and minds without them realizing it. After checking in at the Floating Island

Resort on the Inle Lake on Christmas Eve, eleven of the tourists went for a boat ride to see the sunrise on Christmas morning. Harry Bailley did not join them because he drank heavily the night before and overslept. Unexpectedly, some native Burmese (known as the Karen people and the Lord's Army) led by a young man by the name of Black Spot, mistook one of the group members, fifteen-year-old Rupert, as the legendary savior of their vanishing tribe. Because Rupert demonstrated some tricks with a deck of cards and carried Stephen King's book *Misery*, Black Spot and his fellow men thought he was the Reincarnated One (also known as the Younger White Brother, Lord of Nats) and the book *Misery* was the lost Important Writings. The Karen people had believed in the Younger White Brother for hundreds of years as an important part of their mythology. With the hope that the Reincarnated One could save their tribe from being entirely wiped out by the SLORC (State Law and Order Restoration Council) soldiers, Black Spot brought the tourist group of eleven (four men, five women, and two teenagers) to No Name Place, a secret camp up in the mountains, to meet the rest of the Karen tribe who were hiding from the SLORC soldiers. They pretended that the only bridge connecting their residence and the outside world had fallen and therefore the way out of No Name Place was cut off. As a result, the tourists were marooned in the wild with the Karen tribe.

After word about the tourists going missing on Christmas Day spread, different news channels and organizations tended to connect the event to the political situation of Burma, especially its newly established government. Speculation about the tourists' experience and fate circulated around until the American tourists together with the remaining Karen tribe were rescued from No Name Place on January 16. In the end, the tourists returned to their homes, keeping in touch with one another now and then. The Karens were said to have disappeared after shooting episodes of *Junglemaniacs* with an American film studio, making their way to a refugee camp on the Thai border, and then being transported back to Burma. The novel ends with the truth of Bibi Chen's mysterious death. It turned out that Bibi was not murdered, but accidentally died when she fell from a stool onto her late mother's precious hair comb and was drowned in her own blood.

CHARACTERS, THEMES, AND SETTINGS

Unlike any of her previous novels, Tan portrays a group of characters with very different backgrounds and personalities who are bound together by the Burma Road trip. The medium Karen Lundegaard describes Bibi Chen as "A petite, feisty Chinese woman, opinionated, and hilarious when she didn't intend to be" (*Drowning,* xii). Bibi's character that is "piquant, quirky, often inappropriate, and yet honest" resembles that of Tan's mother, Daisy (http://amytan.net). A well-known socialite during her lifetime, Bibi witnessed her own funeral as an invisible spirit. Around eight hundred people attended the event, including the mayor of San Francisco. Bibi was never beautiful when she was alive but she had an eye for beauty. She knew how to transform her faults into an "effect" so as to make herself unforgettable. She had a style that was "absolutely memorable, as emblematic as the best portraiture of the Sackler collection" (*Drowning,* 13). She thus was known not for beauty but for uniqueness. As Bibi reflected upon her life at her own funeral, she recognized that no one had loved her wholly and desperately even though she had had men as steady companions and enjoyed various degrees of fondness. Growing up in a wealthy family but without parental love, Bibi learned to avoid feelings and emotions. Therefore she never lost control and could not fall madly in love.

The reader gets to know the twelve travelers through Bibi's narrative. Harry Bailley is a forty-two-year-old British-born celebrity dog trainer who has been featured on the television series *The Fido Files.* Upon embarking on the Burma Road trip, Harry was facing a midlife crisis: receding hairline, enlarged prostate, and lack of a soul mate after a divorce and several failed relationships. As a result, he was searching for love and intimacy. During the trip he wooed Marlena Chu but their first night together on Christmas Eve ended in disaster: the romantic candle

A dramatic departure from the themes and subject matter of her previous works of fiction, *Saving Fish from Drowning* demonstrates another dimension of Amy Tan's talent as a writer. The review published in the *San Jose Mercury News* stated: "Tan's imagination and ingenuity are apparent throughout the book, which is chockablock with bright ideas, clever observations, entertaining characters and strong feelings" (http://amytan.net). Tan calls it a book of intentions and morality, in which she adopts fictional devices from a number of genres: murder mystery, romance, picaresque, comic novel, magical realism, fable, myth, police detective, political farce, and so forth (http://amytan.net). It is her hope that readers not only enjoy reading *Saving Fish from Drowning* but also want to ask questions in their own lives about how truth affects intentions, where they find both individual and universal truth, and the importance of having both (http://amytan.net).

caused a fire in Harry's room and both lovers were humiliated when others rushed in to help. Then Harry drank heavily, overslept, and missed the sunrise adventure. He was the first one to report the other missing tourists to the resort management.

Marlena Chu, a woman with a formerly wealthy and powerful family, a Shanghainese birth, a childhood in Sao Paulo, studies at the Sorbonne, and a divorce, is a professional art curator for private collections and corporations. She joined the tourist group with her teenage daughter Esmé. Before leaving China, Esmé secretly adopted a sick puppy and later nursed her to health. After returning from the trip, Marlena and Harry started a relationship.

Roxanne Scarangello, an evolutionary biologist, a Darwin scholar, and a MacArthur fellow, joined the group together with her husband Dwight Massey, a behavioral psychologist who is twelve years her junior and has been her student. At the beginning of their relationship, Dwight worshipped Roxanne. When the group departed from San Francisco, however, the couple was struggling with infertility as well as the growing distance between them. After the trip, Roxanne had a baby son, Lucas, and raised him with Dwight's help.

Mark Moffett, known as Moff, is Harry's friend from their old boarding school days in Switzerland. Moff is also in his forties and divorced. His fifteen-year-old son, Rupert, was mistaken for the Younger White Brother, savior of the Karen people. During their stay at No Name Place, Rupert was both pleased and embarrassed by the special attention bestowed on him by the natives. Heidi Stark, Roxanne's half sister, worried about everything and carried comprehensive medical and emergency supplies for the trip, much of which came in handy. After the trip, Heidi and Moff lived together.

Wendy Brookhyser is a prominent journalist and activist for Free to Speak International, a human rights organization. Her lover, Wyatt Fletcher, who is pleasant yet lacks motivation, joined the trip under the auspices of Wendy's mother, Mary Ellen. In China and Burma, Wendy showed insecurity and sought out Wyatt's attention constantly. Wyatt, on the other hand, was annoyed by Wendy's demanding attitude and tried to keep things under control so that they could enjoy the trip together. After the trip, the couple went their separate ways.

Bennie Trueba y Cela, the newly designated tour leader, is a graphic artist. Bennie had good intentions and liked to please people, but he was not a good choice when it came to leadership. After the trip, Bennie happily reunited with his partner Timothy. Vera Hendricks, director of a large nonprofit foundation, is often included in the Hundred Most Influential Black Women of America. At the age of sixty, Vera is the oldest traveler in the group. After returning home, Vera wrote a book on self-reliance.

Maung Wa Sao, also known as Walter, is the group's tour guide in Burma. A slim young man of twenty-six, Walter has fine features and dark shiny hair and speaks impeccable English. The language has been a boon as well as a curse in his family. Walter's great-great-grandfather worked as an interpreter for the British Raj and was killed in a gunfight. His son went to a secular school for native boys run by British educators, became the first Burmese headmaster, and died of probable heatstroke after a cricket game. Walter's grandfather was a teacher at the mission school. His grandmother, an English-speaking nurse, died in a car accident, leaving behind a husband, three sons, and a daughter. Walter's father, the oldest, became a journalist and a university professor. In 1989 he was arrested for protesting against the military and died in prison. His family history makes Walter wonder frequently what might happen to him one day. The day after the tour group disappeared, he was found unconscious inside an old pagoda near the lake and could not provide any useful information regarding the missing American tourists due to a head injury, concussion, and loss of memory.

Embedded in the novel are critiques of Burma's repressive regime, sympathy for the native Karens who were mistreated and tortured, and questions regarding human rights activists and the media. The government had renamed the country Myanmar, overturned elections by military force, claimed tribal territory as national property, tortured and executed Karens, and placed Aung San Suu Kyi (who won a Nobel Peace Prize) under house arrest. As Black Spot states, to the SLORC soldiers, the Karen tribe was like "goats, animals to be hunted and slaughtered. They would keep hunting them until a SLORC leader's dream had come true: that the only Karen you could see in Burma was stuffed and in the glass case of a museum" (*Drowning,* 311).

Saving Fish from Drowning also addresses the power and problematic issues of the media. Writing with the awareness that the global power of television has been transforming and invading all dimensions of life, Tan emphasizes the importance of fiction for this era to understand people and reality (http://amytan.net). For example, in the remote No Name Place that has no other modern conveniences for everyday life, the Karen people nevertheless have a television set and can watch the *Global News Network*, *Darwin's Fittest*, and other programs in the jungle. After the tourists' disappearance on Christmas Day, 130 international newswires had reported stories by New Year's Day about the eleven missing Americans, the "sexy news." A British independent videographer, Garrett Wyeth, persuaded Harry Bailley to conduct a video interview and sold it to the *Global News Network* for $15,000. As Wyeth stated, "The media makes it happen…. That's how news determines what happens in the world" (*Drowning*, 322). The Myanmar ministers decided to launch a new television series to broadcast the beautiful landscape and rich culture in Burma in order to boost tourism, using the missing tourists as a prelude. The television show *The Fido Files* featuring Harry aired reruns.

DISCUSSION QUESTIONS

- Where does the book title, *Saving Fish from Drowning*, come from? What is the meaning of "saving fish from drowning" in Burmese culture? How does the novel reflect this meaning?
- Discuss the setting of the novel, Burma—its landscape, its people, its cultural traditions, its political situation, the interactions between the natives and the tourists, and the responses to the disappearance of the group of eleven American tourists. What social and political implications are embedded in the story?
- Discuss the romances of the following characters: Harry Bailley and Marlena Chu, Wendy Brookhyser and Wyatt Fletcher, Mark Moffett (Moff) and Heidi Stark. How does the Burma Road trip affect the relationships within each couple? What happens to each couple during the first part of their trip, when they are marooned in the mountains with the native Karens, and then after they return home?
- What role does the media play after the eleven American tourists disappear in Burma on Christmas Day? What implications does the story try to convey?
- Different from Amy Tan's other novels in which characters are usually bound by family, *Saving Fish from Drowning* portrays a group of characters who are not, for the most part, related. Discuss the relationships among the twelve tourists before, during, and after the trip.
- Tan calls *Saving Fish from Drowning* a "comic novel." Find specific examples from the book that represent the "comic" aspects and discuss the humor in the story.

8

OTHER WORKS BY AMY TAN

By 2008, Amy Tan published eight books, including five novels, a book of nonfiction, and two children's books, as well as several short stories and essays. Her writing has won her numerous awards and honors. Some universal themes in Tan's works have struck a chord in many readers' hearts and have attracted much scholarly attention as well. Some of the important themes found in her writing include the complexity of human relationships, especially those in families and between mothers and daughters; the immigrant experience, bicultural heritage, and identity; ethnic exoticism and stereotypes, assimilation, and multiculturalism; female lineage, storytelling, and generational conflict; autobiography versus fiction; and fate versus faith.

The Opposite of Fate: Memories of a Writing Life

The Opposite of Fate: Memories of a Writing Life is Amy Tan's first book of nonfiction. Divided into seven sections—"Fate and Faith," "Changing the Past," "American Circumstances and Chinese Character," "Strong Winds, Strong Influences," "Luck, Chance, and a Charmed Life," "A Choice of Words," and "Hope"—the essays vary in length, subject, and style. These short pieces are the author's reflection on her life, her family, her writing career, and especially her mother's influence. As supplemental readings they help Tan's readers better comprehend her novels and understand her life as a writer.

Released in 2003, this collection of essays received mixed reviews. Among those praising it, a *Booklist* review stated: "Tan is mischievously hilarious and intensely moving. No matter how much readers already revere Tan, their appreciation for her will grow tenfold after experiencing these provocative and unforgettable revelations" (*Fate*, fly page). Another review published in *The Columbus Dispatch* praised Tan's book as "a window into a candid, funny and engaging mind, as well as a provocative meditation on the way stories—and how we tell them—can shape our lives" (*Fate*, fly page). Yet the book also received criticism because several essays had been previously published and that the short pieces address different subject matter and therefore form a disjointed book.

DISCUSSION QUESTIONS

- How does Tan define fate in *The Opposite of Fate*? Do you agree with her definition? Why or why not?
- Discuss the author's bicultural heritage with regard to the title of the book, *The Opposite of Fate*. To what extent do her upbringing and life experience affect her understanding of fate?
- This book includes a number of essays, some of which were previously published. How does the author organize the events, thoughts, experiences, and other details in her life? Do you see a clear structure in the book?
- If you have read any of Tan's novels, how does reading *The Opposite of Fate* change or affect your understanding of her fiction?

THE MOON LADY

Published in 1992 by Macmillan, *The Moon Lady* is Amy Tan's first book for children in collaboration with her friend and award-winning illustrator, Gretchen Schields. The book won the American Library Association's Award for Best Book for Young Adults. The story line adapts the chapter titled "The Moon Lady" from Tan's best-selling novel, *The Joy Luck Club*. The text is accompanied by illustrations in color. The book begins with three children—Maggie, Lily, and June—spending a rainy day in the apartment of their Nai-nai (meaning "grandma"). Nai-nai tells the story of one Moon Festival in China when she was a seven-year-old girl, called Ying-ying.

On the fifteenth day of the eighth month in the Chinese lunar calendar, Ying-ying's family celebrated the Moon Festival, like many other Chinese families. Her father rented a boat so that the whole family could enjoy the holiday on the Tai Lake. After getting dressed in the morning in her new outfit made specifically for the occasion, Ying-ying was excited about the possibility of seeing the legendary Moon Lady (also known as Lady Chang-o) who lives on the moon and is said to be able to fulfill people's secret wishes. Ying-ying's morning was filled with eating moon cakes, chasing a dragonfly, and playing with her shadow before she went to the lake with her family. On the boat, they had a big lunch feast. Afterward, when others napped through the hottest hours of the day, Ying-ying wandered through the boat into the kitchen where live eels were sliced in preparation for the dinner soup. Since she stood by closely to watch, Ying-ying's nice silk jacket and pants were stained with eel blood. Her nursemaid scolded her and made her take off her stained clothes. When evening came and the firecrackers exploded, Ying-ying, now wearing her cotton undergarment, lost her balance and fell into the water. Later she was saved, but she could not find her family. As she went on to watch a shadow play of the Moon Lady, Ying-ying shouted her true secret wish: she wished to be found and to reunite with her family. The book concludes with Ying-ying, now a grandma, telling Maggie, Lily, and June that she was indeed found at last. Together they danced under the full moon.

DISCUSSION QUESTIONS

- Discuss the narrative structure of *The Moon Lady*: how the book introduces the main story line, how the plot develops, and what the point of view is.
- Analyze the character Ying-ying through her actions and her interactions with other characters.
- Describe the Moon Festival celebration in terms of food, people's dressing style, holiday activities, and other aspects that you find in the book.

THE CHINESE SIAMESE CAT

Three years after her cat Sagwa died at the age of twenty-one, Amy Tan collaborated with Gretchen Schields again for their second picture book for children, *The Chinese Siamese Cat,* published by Macmillan in 1994

The book opens with Ming Miao telling the story about their great ancestor, a Chinese cat named Sagwa (meaning "mellow head," "silly") to her kittens before sending them out into the world. Sagwa's parents, Mama Miao and Baba Miao, lived in the House of the Foolish Magistrate who took charge of making the rules for subjects in his province. The Magistrate used Mama Miao and Baba Miao's pointy-tipped tails as writing brushes to issue rules. Sagwa was a kitten that always made her way into trouble. After the Magistrate made Mama Miao write the new rule that "People must not sing until the sun goes down," Sagwa leaped into the inkpot and accidentally stained the new rule, changing the words to "People must sing until the sun goes down." When people sang happily, praising the Magistrate, he was deeply touched and decided to reward his people and his cats.

Tan read the story of Sagwa at the Louise M. Davies Symphony Hall in San Francisco accompanied by a full orchestra while Schields's illustrations were projected on a large screen. Later an animated series for PBS, titled *Sagwa*, adapted this book targeting particularly five- to eight-year-old children. This PBS series, aired worldwide from 2001 to 2003, aimed to help children explore ancient Chinese culture as well as different customs around the globe (http://pbskids.org/sagwa/caregivers/index.html). It won an Emmy nomination and Parents' Choice Award for Best Television Program for Children.

DISCUSSION QUESTIONS

- Family connections to ancestors is a recurring theme in Tan's novels. What role does family play in *The Chinese Siamese Cat*? How does the author write about family similarly or differently for child readers compared to in novels for adults?

- Analyze the character of Sagwa. How is she different from other kittens in the story?

- The story is set in ancient China. What are the universal themes the reader can identify, no matter what cultural background he or she comes from?

- Chinese American critic Sheng-mei Ma remarks: "Schields's graphics are an amalgamation of the style of chinoiserie, on the one hand, and of ethnic stereotypes of Chinese, on the other. Both sources for Schields's creation are Orientalized images of China" (2000, 95). Do you agree with his opinion about the illustrations of *The Moon Lady* and *The Chinese Siamese Cat*? Why or why not?

9

TODAY'S ISSUES IN AMY TAN'S WORK

Contemporary American Literature and Culture

It would not be an exaggeration to say that Amy Tan has influenced an entire generation of readers and writers (Shea and Wilchek, 17). To her, stories are about the search for balance in life (*The Opposite of Fate,* 302), a theme that has a universal appeal to general readers. Among the writers who have introduced Chinese American and by extension Asian American experience to mainstream audiences, Tan often is discussed together with other Chinese American writers such as Jade Snow Wong and Maxine Hong Kingston. The multiple story lines in *The Joy Luck Club* are "beautifully interwoven with legend and memory, archetype and longing. Like Maxine Hong Kingston's brilliant *The Woman Warrior,* published more than a decade ago, these tales blend the mythical and the mundane, and the endings are often astonishing connections of the two" (Cheng 1989, 12). Collectively these writers have helped pave the way for Asian American literature and literary studies.

Several years before Tan made her debut in the literary world, Elaine H. Kim's groundbreaking book, *Asian American Literature: An Introduction to the Writings and Social Context* (1982), directed academic attention to the field of Asian American literature. *The Joy Luck Club* was published at a time when general interest in ethnic experience was on the rise in America. Barbara Kramer has called Tan "a trailblazer for other Chinese-American writers" (98). While reading *The Joy Luck Club,* the reader is "being reminded not just of the nightmarishness of being a woman in traditional China, but of the enormity of the confusing mental journey Chinese emigrants had to make" (Schell, 28). The popularity and critical aftermath of *The Joy Luck Club* "have contributed greatly to the recognition and validation of Asian American fiction in American literature" (Dong b, 1205). By exploring questions that arise in her life and interest her (Seaman, 257), Tan investigates the larger questions of life while adding a significant literary voice to contemporary American culture.

There has been some criticism of Tan's portrayal of China, Chinese traditions, and Chinese American culture in her novels. For example, Ruth Maxey criticizes Kingston and Tan's configuration of China as "an imaginary homeland replete with recurrent, often negative stereotypes" (Maxey, 1). Sheng-mei Ma has pointed out that by integrating "1990s realism with Orientalist discourse" and ethnicizing the primitive in *The Hundred Secret Senses*, Tan earned "success among white, middle-class, 'mainstream' readers living in the climate of the New Age (Ma 2001, 30). Ma claims that for Tan, "Chinese dogs" and "Chinese gods" are the same, both reenacting the "Orientalism fantasies of her massive 'mainstream' following" (Ma 2001, 43). Susan Muaddi Darraj, however, has defended Tan against the charge of a stereotypical depiction of China: "All cultures have dark periods in their history, but to write about those times does not mean that a writer hates or is trying to falsely depict that culture. At the same time, other writers have portrayed the culture wrongly in the past, which makes some people, like Amy Tan's critics, more sensitive to these depictions" (66). A friend of Tan's, a reporter who writes on literature, once told the author that she should be grateful for any attention, good or bad: "The media need an angle. Culture is the angle. A new wave in Asian-American literature is the angle…. They're not going to devote column inches to talking about the beauty of their prose, the cleverness of their characterization. That's not topical. That's not interesting" (*Fate*, 312). Tan's works have attracted much attention.

Tan was surprised that *The Joy Luck Club* received "good feedback from literary people from China and Taiwan; a woman who had come from Beijing ten years ago said, 'There are women in that book who are just like my mother'" (Henderson, 20). The price that Tan has paid for the overwhelming success of her novel is the loss of a sense of "comfort." She has said:

> The success of *The Joy Luck Club* was the kind of experience where one could say, "You have absolutely nothing to complain about. This is all so wonderful." That's true. But there was a part of me that was very angry, and I didn't understand why at

first.... When I woke up, I realized what I had lost: this old feeling of comfort. (Tan, "Amy Tan," in *Writers Dreaming*, 287–88)

Such a feeling is shared by many authors whose names become widely known to readers and critics when they first enter the literary world.

With the growing scholarship on translation in relation to cultural exchange, Tan's works have brought attention in terms of the cultural translation of the parental past in constructing the future. Often compared to Maxine Hong Kingston's acclaimed *The Woman Warrior*, Tan's *The Hundred Secret Senses* and *The Bonesetter's Daughter* tell intriguing family tales crossing different time periods and geographical locations and incorporate ghosts as cultural symbols. The main characters usually function as cultural translators who provide a bridge to a China that is situated in the past and is remote from America.

Tan noticed the tendency among reviewers and scholars to impose questionable motivations on her through speculation about how and why she writes her works. She remarks: "Reviewers and students have educated me not only about how I write, but about why I write. Apparently, I wish to capture the immigrant experience, to demystify Chinese culture, to show the differences between Chinese and American culture, to pave the way for other Asian-American writers—and I have a whole host of other equally noble motivations" (*Fate,* 304). In particular, Tan has addressed two issues related to such speculations. First of all, as she has confessed repeatedly, she writes for more self-serving reasons: she writes for herself and writes stories about life as she has misunderstood it. Secondly, Tan is quite alarmed whenever others assume that her personal, specific, and fictional stories are representative of Chinese Americans and by extension Asian Americans (*Fate,* 304, 305). Voicing her concern about the ethnic ghettoized label imposed on her works, Tan consciously calls for a broader view of literature and literary works.

In her essay "Required Reading and Other Dangerous Subjects," Tan addresses the problematic grouping of "writers of color" and instead positions herself as an American writer:

> If I had to give myself any sort of label, I would have to say I am an American writer. I am Chinese by racial heritage. I am Chinese-American by family and social upbringing. But I believe that what I write is American fiction by virtue of the fact that I live in this country and my emotional sensibilities,

assumptions, and obsessions are largely American. My characters may be largely Chinese-American, but I think Chinese-Americans are part of America. (*Fate*, 310)

Thus Tan's vision of twenty-first century American literature is "democratic in its inclusion of many colorful voices, men and women, gay and straight, of all ethnicities and races" (*Fate*, 321). She resists the racial and ethnic labels imposed on her as well as other writers.

Tan's concern extends beyond her books to literature in general. Realizing the fact that works written by ethnic authors including herself may be read more likely as sociology, ethnography, politics, ideology, and cultural lesson plans in narrative form rather than as literary fiction, Tan points out the danger in this trend that usually comes under the euphoric umbrella of multiculturalism: "It disturbs me ... it terrifies me when I hear people dictating what literature must do and mean and say. And it infuriates me when people use the 'authority' of their race, gender, and class to stipulate who should write what, and why. The prohibitions come in many forms.... The mandates are just as strong" (*Fate*, 308–9). Tan has repeatedly expressed her concern about the inevitable ethnic labels associated with her works as well as many other writers:

> Placing on writers the responsibility to represent a culture is an onerous burden. Someone who writes fiction is not necessarily writing a depiction of any generalized group, they're writing a very specific story. There's also a danger in balkanizing literature, as if it should be read as sociology, or politics, or that it should answer questions like "What does *The Hundred Secret Senses* have to teach us about Chinese culture?" As opposed to treating it as literature—as a story, language, memory. ("The Spirit Within, Salon Interview: Amy Tan.")

Tan feels it is problematic to read her works as representative of Chinese American experience; her works include much more diversity within them. The stories she writes incorporate a number of themes and topics that are not necessarily specific to Chinese and Chinese American families, even though her works mainly feature Chinese American characters.

In the commencement address she delivered at Simmons College in Boston in 2003 (whose edited version is collected in *The Opposite of Fate*, 291–98), Tan gave the graduating classes five writing tips: avoid clichés; avoid generalizations; find your own voice; show compassion; and ask the important questions. As a successful writer, Tan pays much attention to language in particular. She has told her readers: "I choose my words carefully, with much anguish. They are, each and every one, significant to me, by virtue of their meaning, their tone, their place in the sentence, their sound and rhythm in dialogue or narrative, their specific associations with something deeply personal and often secretly ironic in my life" (*Fate,* 301–2). Many readers and critics have noted the accessibility of Tan's language in her novels, that she tends to tell intricate stories, relay complex themes, and register important social and cultural issues in a "simple" style. Yet the author makes it clear that her seemingly effortless style is actually the result of an "anguished" process of searching, musing, selecting, and revising. Such a reader-friendly writing style, in its facilitation of the natural flow of the narrative in Tan's fiction and nonfiction, helps account for her popularity among contemporary American writers.

WOMEN'S ISSUES

With its primary focus on women's lives told in women's voices, *The Joy Luck Club* not surprisingly invites analysis from a feminist vantage point. Such an initiative has been carried on with Tan's three subsequent novels—*The Kitchen God's Wife, The Hundred Secret Senses*, and *The Bonesetter's Daughter*—by scholars as well as reviewers and the general public. For instance, *The Kitchen God's Wife* has been studied together with texts by Louise Erdrich, Mary Gordon, Toni Morrison, Marge Piercy, and Jane Smiley in the context of domesticity in postfeminist novels (Cooperman, 1999).

Women's Issues in Amy Tan's The Joy Luck Club (2008), edited by Gary Wiener, collects more than a dozen essays that discuss Tan's novel with a focus on gender identity, female lineage, and other social issues with regard to women. These previously published essays address a variety of topics: generational and cultural differences; spatial, temporal, and spiritual journeys; parental expectations versus adolescent rebellion; storytelling and reconciliation; female empowerment; gender and ethnic stereotypes; and feminism in the new millennium. This volume is part of the Social Issues in Literature Series, launched by Thomson Gale. The series includes volumes on F. Scott Fitzgerald's *The Great Gatsby* (1925), Harper Lee's *To Kill a Mockingbird* (1960), and Maya Angelou's *I Know Why the Caged Bird Sings* (1969).

The Joy Luck Club, The Kitchen God's Wife, and *The Bonesetter's Daughter* have made meaningful contributions to the literary representation of women's lives and relationships. The frequent references to "traditional beliefs and practices such as astrology, *wu-hsing*, and *feng shui* emphasize the distance between the Chinese mothers and their American-born daughters" in Tan's novels (Hamilton, 143). Analyzing the "joy luck mothers and Coca-Cola daughters" in Tan's novel, Wendy Ho states

> [T]he recognition and reclamation of the social and emotional bonds between a Chinese mother and her daughter, in counterpoint to the images and definitions of women in interlocking patriarchal, capitalist, and imperialist discourses, can be a form of political and historical power and subversion not only for women but for their families and communities. Such a perspective makes visible women's everyday activities and locations in negotiating survival and resistance. To name and define each other—for ourselves, by ourselves, and of ourselves—is a return to the complex dynamics of agency at the multiple social sites we intimately inhabit as women. (Ho 1999, 188–89)

By introducing and analyzing personal experiences, these novels also show what is beyond the women characters: "the reality of the confrontation of two cultures, of two generations, that can finally be reconciled in the new and final destiny of the immigration process" (López Morell, 77). Thus Tan's fiction resonates with many readers from different cultural backgrounds.

The Hundred Secret Senses shifts its focus from the mother-daughter relationship to the bond between two sisters who "work out issues of identity and difference with each other" (Yu, 347). This novel, together with other texts by contemporary women writers such as Cristina Garcia's *The Aguero Sisters* (1997), "not only challenge the validity and general application of the traditionally idealistic sisterhood but also adumbrate a radically alternative figuration of sisterhood" (Yu, 347). In portraying the dynamics between the half sisters Kwan Li and Olivia Bishop in a compelling family drama with a sense of humor, Tan unfolds the complex process of characters searching for identity, balancing their cultural differences, and discovering and developing their bonds in multiple parameters. Instead of providing answers about interracial and multicultural relationships between sisters, Tan's novel raises a series of questions with regard to "current estimations of sister relationships and women's communities" within the large context of the feminist movement and ethnic literature (Yu, 359). Her writing not only is compelling but also invites further contemplation of these social issues.

In the Classroom

Since publication of *The Joy Luck Club*, Amy Tan's name remains fixed on classroom reading lists in secondary schools, colleges, universities, and other academies. There are many reasons for her strong acceptance among teachers and students. Her voice resonates with students, and by telling stories through fiction and nonfiction she helps teachers and students understand their own struggles, explore their own lives, and find ways to tell their own stories (Shea and Wilchek, xv, xvii). Tan's belief in "the transformative power of narrative" (Shea and Wilchek, 1) is a common thread in her life and writing. Tan's popularity in classrooms is reflected in the large number of study guides for her works that exist in print and electronic resources, such as *Amy Tan in the Classroom: "The Art of Invisible Strength"* (2005) included in the National Council of Teachers of English High School Literature Series. The unique structure of *The Joy Luck Club* is one aspect responsible for its popularity among students and teachers. Organizing her book of sixteen stories in a structure that is interrelated and emotional, Tan provides "natural breaking points for reading assignments and discussion" (Shea and Wilchek, 20). *The Joy Luck Club* is not only a useful text for literature classes due to its striking story line, unique structure, remarkable characters, and complex cultural themes, but it is also a good resource to teach writing and social issues.

More and more teachers face challenges posed by rapidly changing demographics in the United States and growing language obstacles for a number of students whose native tongue is not English. A research project sponsored by the University of California at Irvine and the California Writing Project was conducted with ninth grade students at Century High School in Santa Ana Unified School District to find out how profoundly students of diverse cultural backgrounds reacted to "The Moon Lady" from *The Joy Luck Club*. This particular story was singled out because "it lent itself so well to character analysis and the teaching of analytical writing" (Olson and Clark, 86). In teaching analytical writing in a multicultural class, the teachers designed their instructional scaffold to "promote creativity and fluency first and then to help students impose form and correctness" (Olson and Clark, 96). This research provided strong evidence that "The Moon Lady" helped students improve their reading and writing abilities as well as their understanding of their own identities (Olson and Clark, 98). This is just one example of how Tan's writing has the potential to shape America's growing multicultural reality through school curricula.

One of the challenges facing teachers in the new millennium was revealed in a 2004 National Endowment for the Arts (NEA) report, "Reading at Risk: A Survey of Literary Reading in America" (available at http://www.nea.gov/pub/ReadingAtRisk.pdf). NEA's chairman, Dana Gioia, said that the report "identified a critical decline in reading for pleasure among American adults. The Big Read aims to address this issue directly by providing citizens with the opportunity to read and discuss a single book within their communities." *The Joy Luck Club* was chosen by NEA for its Big Read program, which inspires people across the country to pick up a good book, listen to radio programs, watch video profiles, and read essays about classic authors. Other books in the Big Read program include: *Bless Me, Ultima* (1972), *My Antonia* (1918), *The Great Gatsby* (1925), *A Farewell to Arms* (1929), *To Kill a Mockingbird* (1960), *The Grapes of Wrath* (1939), and *The Age of Innocence* (1920), to list only a few.

In order to spark students' interest in reading and motivate their response to language and literature, teachers have to choose literary texts carefully. *The Joy Luck Club* stays on many favorite reading lists partly because of its rich content and the different ways teachers can approach the text. For example, Shea and Wilchek illustrate how they use "interrupted reading as introduction to text," "graphic organizers for character analysis," and "close reading in context" in teaching students to analyze Tan's novel effectively (33–49). Then they encourage students' discussion and further exploration of four challenges that they have identified in Tan's novel: a problematic narrative structure, eight complex characters, unfamiliar cultural context, and gender bias (Shea and Wilchek, 50). They also point out that using the film adaptation is "another way to engage students in analysis of the novel, critical thinking, and even close reading of the written text" (Shea and Wilchek, 67). The film's R rating, however, disqualifies it for classroom screening in most public high schools. Nevertheless, selected film clips can provide useful companions to textual analysis.

There are a number of print and electronic resources for teachers and students, most of which are study guides to *The Joy Luck Club*. The chapter "Amy Tan on the Internet," includes an overview of Internet resources. Other useful resources include: CliffsNotes to *The Joy Luck Club* by Laurie Neu Rozakis (1994); Marion B. Hoffman's *The Joy Luck Club: A Unit Plan* (1999); the Gale Group's study guides to Tan's "Two Kinds," *The Joy Luck Club*, and *The Kitchen God's Wife*. MAXnotes, published by Research and Education Association, has a volume on *The Joy Luck Club* written by Carla J. Beard and illustrated by Ann Tango-Schurmann. In addition, a number of teacher-scholars have published articles discussing pedagogy, experiences, and suggestions for teaching Amy Tan in school classrooms. For example, Roger W. Shanley's article "Novel Choices, Pun Intended," explains why *The Joy Luck Club* is one of the most desirable books for students based on his own teaching experience. Marlene Koenig's article "With a Little Bit of Joy and Luck" outlines her methodology and pedagogy in teaching Tan's novel. Both Frances A. Nadeau's and Judith Hayn and Deborah Sherrill's aforementioned articles address Tan's debut book in the context of teaching young adult literature.

DISCUSSION QUESTIONS

- Discuss how Tan handles mother-daughter bonds as well as conflicts in her novels *The Joy Luck Club*, *The Kitchen God's Wife*, and *The Hundred Secret Senses*. To what degree are these relationships specific to Chinese American families and to what degree are they universal regardless of one's ethnic or cultural background?
- Discuss the female characters in *The Joy Luck Club* within the social context of the civil rights movement and the feminist movement in the United States in the 1960s. What do they tell the reader about American women in general and Chinese women in particular?
- In comparison to its female characters, *The Joy Luck Club* seems to have a limited and sometimes negative depiction of its male characters. Do you think the lack of a male voice and the limitation of the portrayal of men are strengths or weaknesses of the novel? Why or why not?
- Discuss Tan's view of being called a "writer of color." Why does she consider such a label problematic? Do you agree with her? Why or why not?
- How does Tan reveal the serious political situation in Burma in her "comic novel," *Saving Fish from Drowning*? How does her fiction reflect the influence of Western human rights activism on the Burmese regime and the Burmese people?
- How does Tan portray the role of the media in contemporary life in *Saving Fish from Drowning*, especially during the search for the missing tourists?
- Discuss how Tan's writing has been used in high school and college curricula. How do instructors teach her works and how do students understand them? What is the author's view of multiculturalism in school curricula in the United States?

- Discuss how Tan's writing reflects the writing tips that she gave to the graduating class at Simmons College in Boston in 2003: avoid clichés; avoid generalizations; find your own voice; show compassion; and ask the important questions (*Fate*, 295–97). How useful are these tips for your own writing?

10

POP CULTURE IN AMY
TAN'S WORK

Many readers, reviewers, and critics came to know the name Amy Tan shortly after the publication of *The Joy Luck Club* in 1989. With the impressive sales numbers of her first book as well as overwhelmingly positive response to it, Tan quickly became not only a rising star among. contemporary fiction writers but also in American popular culture. Susan Muaddi Darraj's book *Amy Tan* (2007), for example, was published in Chelsea House's Asian Americans of Achievement series. Biographies published in the same series include that of Bruce Lee, Michelle Kwan, Yo-Yo Ma, Vera Wang, among others, all of whom are well-known names in American popular culture.

FILM AND STAGE ADAPTATIONS OF *THE JOY LUCK CLUB*

Even though Tan considered herself "an unlikely person to get involved with filmmaking" since she always preferred to daydream about characters of her own making (*The Opposite of Fate*, 176), her overwhelmingly successful novel opened another door for her. The remarkable acceptance of *The Joy Luck Club* brought Tan attention from the American filmmaking business. Her initial concern about turning her book into a film led her to decline such offers. Tan worried about the possibility that the silver screen might reinforce racial stereotypes in portraying the Chinese American characters in her story, as the American film industry had done in the past. Her mind did not change until August 1989 when she met Wayne Wang, a Chinese American director who earned a reputation for his films *Chan Is Missing* (1982), *Dim Sum: A Little Bit of Heart* (1985), and *Eat a Bowl of Tea* (1989). Their conversation eased Tan's anxiety and marked the beginning of their collaboration for the film adaptation of *The Joy Luck Club*. Wayne Wang, Amy Tan, and screenwriter Ronald Bass formed a team of three and decided to "seek creative control" of the filmmaking process (*Fate,* 182). Even though she knew nothing about script writing, Tan quickly acquired knowledge and skills about the new genre and co-wrote the screenplay with Bass. Because Tan and her teammates insisted on taking creative control, an earlier negotiation with a filmmaking company fell through.

After reaching an agreement with Disney Studio's chairman Jeffrey Katzenberg and with Kathryn Galan and Henry Huang of Disney and its Hollywood Pictures in March 1992, the filming began in October of the same year. The film was shot in Richmond, Virginia, and Guilin, China. Tan served as the co-producer for the film as well. The film not only incorporates a number of her family photos, including those of her late father and elder brother, but it also casts Tan, her mother, Ronald Bass, and some of the real-life Joy Luck Club aunts as extras. Tan documents the preproduction process and the film's shooting in the United States and China in vivid detail in an essay in her book *The Opposite of Fate*. Looking back, she considers her involvement in the filmmaking process a valuable and enjoyable experience in multiple ways.

Despite the fact that the film adaptation cast mostly Asian American actors and was about Chinese Americans without famous stars, *The Joy Luck Club* received critical and popular acclaim when released in theaters in 1993. It was short-listed for the British Academy of Film and Television Arts (BAFTA) Film Award, Best Screenplay Adaptation, as well as for the Writers Guild of America Award, Best Screenplay Adaptation. The film is now available on DVD.

Most viewers are deeply touched by the striking story line and the characters in the film. In academia, however, scholarly criticism on the film adaptation is mixed. Suzanne D. Green's article "Thematic Deviance or Poetic License? The Filming of *The Joy Luck Club*" praises the value and success of the film, yet points to the modifications that harm some of the important thematic elements of the novel; for example, the double jeopardy and duality of the women's objectification; the age-old Chinese ideal of keeping one's "face"; and the usage of the marriage plot device as empowerment for second generation women of Chinese heritage (211–12). In her close reading of the film together with the novel, Green points out that despite its moving and beautiful cinematic designs and its close approximation to the original text, the film fails to effectively communicate the important thematic messages embedded in Tan's novel that helped it enter the top book lists of the late twentieth century (211).

Similarly, Robert Mielke considers the film production of *The Joy Luck Club* to be of lesser quality than the novel (68). Mielke's comparative study of the film and novel addresses the "defensible choices" by the playwrights and director that reflect their desire to reduce the complexities of the characters and their interest in further connecting each mother with her daughter (69, 70). Nonetheless, he notes that the filmmakers' strategy—"to retell the novel as a universal story of mothers and daughters, for a mass audience, in a popular film" (Mielke, 75)—proved to be effective. Even though some of the alterations are praiseworthy—for example, the clearer structural arrangement and the characters' interaction in a frame tale—overall the adaptation is "a simplified version of a more complex novel, a translation for American popular culture" (Mielke, 74–75).

Some critics question the film's representation of Chinese and Chinese Americans. For example, George Tseo has discussed the flaws as well as merits of the film *The Joy Luck Club* as "perils of transcultural translation." Identifying himself as a Chinese American, Tseo criticizes the dialogues of Tan's characters as "stereotypically wooden and metaphorical," through which "the Chinese culture is misrepresented." Such distortions have been deepened even further in the film adaptation (Tseo, 339, 341). At the same time, Tseo praises the family bonds represented in Tan's novel as well as in the film:

> Ultimately, *The Joy Luck Club* is about mothers and daughters. It is in this realm that the story makes its greatest positive contribution; it is here the book is so enjoyable and moving. The truth conveyed by Tan shone through even the movie's thin characterization, which may be why so many young women left the theaters in tears. To them the scenes must have triggered self-recognition. (Tseo, 343)

Overall, scholarly criticism of the film adaptation points to the alteration of the narrative structure and characters' interactions which make the film's storytelling flow better and present a friendlier organization for the viewers yet reduce the complexity embedded in the novel. Clips from the film *The Joy Luck Club* have been used in high school and college classrooms in the United States. This powerful adaptation "affords students an opportunity to see a novel they've studied come to life on the screen and to witness the author's hand in shaping its creation" (Shea and Wilchek, 67). Many teachers find that teaching Tan's novel together with film clips sparks discussion and enhances the learning experience.

After making the film *The Joy Luck Club*, Wayne Wang, Ronald Bass, and Tan received a contract to make a film adaptation of her successful second novel, *The Kitchen God's Wife*. But after some consideration, Tan decided to return to her life of fiction writing. The team of three has talked about the possibility of filming an original screenplay in the future if the right opportunity comes (*Fate*, 204).

The Joy Luck Club also has been adapted into plays and staged in the United States and overseas. Susan Kim's stage adaptation of Tan's novel had its world premiere in 1993. A collaboration of Shanghai People's Art Theater in China and the Long Wharf Theatre in New Haven, Connecticut, the production was staged in Shanghai in Mandarin translation and then in Hong Kong. Kim's play also was performed at the Long Wharf Theatre in English in 1997. In addition, the play was staged by Margaret Brooker, founder of Seattle's Intiman Theatre, on the West Coast. In his review of the West Coast Premiere of the two-and-a-half-hour play *The Joy Luck Club*, Richard Connema remarked that "[t]he performance was strong, particularly the four Chinese mothers.... The play does recapture some of the fire and warmth of Tan's original creation" (http://www.talkinbroadway.com/regional/sanfran/s20.html). This play also was part of the 1998–99 season of TheatreWorks.

In 1999, another production of Susan Kim's play with a different cast premiered at the Pan Asian Repertory Theatre in New York. Directed by Tisa Chang, the play's popularity among audiences and critics led to its production off Broadway at the Julia Miles Theater in 2007. The performances were received so warmly that the performance run was extended by one week ("*The Joy Luck Club* Extends by One Week"). As the director put it, "[t]ranscending nationality, culture and age barriers, *The Joy Luck Club* may be the most successful Asian American fiction of the last quarter-century. It's an Asian American classic and we would like to introduce it to the new generation of artists and audiences" (Visaya). The creative team and cast for the production by the Pan Asian Repertory Theatre were mostly Asian Americans.

After these first productions of Susan Kim's stage adaptation, interest in *The Joy Luck Club* grew. Seattle-based playwright, director, actor, stage manager, and designer David Hsieh adapted *The Joy Luck Club* as a two-act stage play and directed its production. In 2003, Hsieh's adaptation had its world premiere and a five-week run at Seattle's Repertory Actors Theatre. This theatrical adaptation of Tan's novel also was presented in Texas and received international acclaim (http://www.react theatre.org/artist/davidhsieh.html). Respecting Tan as one of his favorite authors, Hsieh insisted that "the relationships between husbands and wives, mothers and daughters, those human stories are what speak to me" amid the specific cultural tensions between first and second generations of Chinese families portrayed in Tan's book (Truzzi). It took Hsieh eighteen months to search for adaptation permission rights and another eight months to create a script and develop staging that adopts a number of Asian theatre techniques, including shadow puppetry (Truzzi). Because of its sensitive and intriguing storytelling of generational relations in immigrant families, *The Joy Luck Club* has had a significant influence on American popular culture and remains popular worldwide today almost two decades after its initial publication.

STAGE AND TELEVISION ADAPTATIONS OF AMY TAN'S OTHER WORKS

PBS created an animated television series, *Sagwa, The Chinese Siamese Cat*, designed particularly for children five to eight years old. The program was based on Amy Tan and Gretchen Schields's book for children, *The Chinese Siamese Cat*. Each PBS episode contains two eleven-minute animated adventures and features a mini-documentary of real children sharing their hobbies, music, special festivals, foods, and neighborhoods. This PBS series helps children explore ancient Chinese culture as well as different customs around the globe. Through the adventures of the hilarious cat Sagwa, child viewers not only acquire familiarity with cultural differences and similarities in various regions, but also have the opportunity to build their skills in dealing with common childhood difficulties such as peer pressure and solving problems among friends. The PBS Web site states that this show addresses two things in particular: "modeling strategies for dealing with the personal and social issues children face as they grow into a variety of new roles" and "exposing children to elements of cultures other than their own and showing that children all over share many of the same interests and emotions" (http://pbskids.org/sagwa/caregivers/index.html). The PBS project is a collaboration on the part of its creators in Montreal, New York, San Francisco, and Virginia, including Tan and Schields. Tan served as creative consultant for the television series, which was nominated for an Emmy Award,

It aired from 2001 to 2003 in the United States, the United Kingdom, Singapore, China, and other regions. Activities for children and games related to this show, as well as information about the making of this program, are available on the PBS Web site at http://pbskids.org/sagwa/.

In 2006, the Word for Word Performing Arts Company in San Francisco, California, produced a stage play, *Immortal Heart*, based on Amy Tan's story of the same title originally published in *The New Yorker* in 2000. Narrated by Lu Ling, the story is about the life of her birth mother, Precious Auntie, and her own experience in the Immortal Heart village south of Peking. This story was later incorporated into Tan's novel *The Bonesetter's Daughter*. The play was directed by Delia MacDougall and received favorable reviews from critics. For example, Richard Connema called the performance "a passionate production" with period costumes that are "eye appealing" (http://talkinbroadway.com/regional/sanfran/s508.html). Chad Jones's essay published in the *Oakland Tribune* stated: "Sadness pervades 'Immortal Heart,' although the storytelling is so deft and so lovely that the sadness is somewhat cushioned. Director Delia MacDougall and her nine-member ensemble work wonders with Tan's prose, which tends toward the prosaic in the latter part of the story" (http://findarticles.com/p/articles/mi_qn4176/is_20040812/ai_n14580336).

Founded in 1993 by Susan Harloe and JoAnne Winter, Word for Word is a program at The Z Space Studio that stages short stories by performing every word the author wrote in them. The program employs more than a hundred San Francisco Bay Area theater professionals and attracts more than 20,000 people to public performances each year. As its Web site states, its goals are "to excite people about the written word, to inspire them to read more, to create new audiences for the theatre, and to share the world's diverse cultures and stories" (http://www.zspace.org/wordforword.htm). As one of Word for Word's touring productions, *Immortal Heart* was performed in different cities in the United States and France with success.

From September 13 to October 3, 2008, the San Francisco Opera staged a production of *The Bonesetter's Daughter*, with music by Stewart Wallace, libretto by Amy Tan and Michael Korie, and directed by Chen Shi-Zheng. The San Francisco Opera Web site states:

> Adapted from the best-selling novel by beloved Bay Area author Amy Tan, this world premiere tells a resonant story of belated intergenerational understanding that leads to emotional

healing.... Composer Stewart Wallace (*Harvey Milk*) incorporates the timbres and textures of Chinese music into his highly expressive and lyrical score—an American opera with roots in China. (http://sfopera.com/o/265.asp)

The composer Stewart Wallace's Web site describes the opera this way:

> *The Bonesetter's Daughter* is a multi-generational family epic that explores one family's history through three generations of mothers and daughters. The opera is set in China during the years before the Communist revolution, framed by the memories and forgotten history of an elderly Chinese mother in present-day San Francisco. The story sweeps from fable-like past to factual present, from Chinese village to urban America. Shifting times and locales are linked by a recurring quartet of women: a girl, a young woman, a mother and an ageless, ghost-spirit known as Precious Auntie. They are the bones of this family throughout time and become the mothers and daughters in each generation. (http://www.harveymilkopera.com/harvey_milk.htm?/htm/txt_a10.htm)

According to San Francisco Opera's Web site, Amy Tan wrote her first libretto "with an eye towards its emotional layers, condensing and heightening the original story and freely borrowing from her other novels and personal history." The Web site also said that Tan and Wallace had traveled over the past three years to China to do research on village funerals, music of ethnic minorities, and Chinese opera in different regions. The opera incorporated a Beijing Opera percussion section and two *suona* (Chinese double-reeded trumpet). The production team included many Chinese artists. This opera runs for two hours and forty minutes, including an intermission that is sung in English with English supertitles. The *San Francisco Chronicle* lauded: "*The Bonesetter's Daughter* explodes onto the stage ... and the resultant air of excitement never really subsides ... beautiful and richly affecting ... a new opera in which musical characterization, dramatic clarity and theatrical vigor combine to form an arresting and vividly memorable experience" (http://sfopera.com/p/?mID=220). The *New York Times* called it "a work of total theater," which "will surely touch many people" (http://sfopera.com/p/?mID=220). Readers can read an overview, synopsis, pre-opera talks, events related to the opera, Opera Guild preview lectures, and Opera Guild Insight Panel Discussions, and also view a photo gallery and selected scenes from the production at the San Francisco Opera Web site: http://sfopera.com/o/265.asp.

The Joy Luck Club, *The Kitchen God's Wife*, *The Hundred Secret Senses*, and *The Opposite of Fate* are available as audiobooks, read by the author herself. Commenting on the abridged audio version of *The Kitchen God's Wife*, the reviewer for *The Midwest Book Review* claims: "Tan herself reads an exceptionally well-done abridged version of her story of Winnie Louie and Helen Kwong, who find their confidences shattered. This is more than a story about family relationships at a cross-roads: it captures the essence of Chinese heritage and culture" (http://www.tuvy.com/resource/books/k/Kitchen_Gods_Wife.html). Tan also performed as the narrator with the San Francisco Symphony and the Hollywood Bowl Orchestra that played an original score for *Sagwa* by composer Nathan Wang (http://amytan.net). In addition, Tan appeared as herself in the animated television series *The Simpsons*. In one of the episodes, Lisa Simpson goes to a book fair to meet all her favorite authors and Amy Tan is one of them.

THE ROCK BOTTOM REMAINDERS

In November 1991, Kathi Kamen Goldmark founded a rock 'n' roll band of high-profile authors called the Rock Bottom Remainders. According to the band's Web site, it "includes some of today's most shining literary lights. Between them, they've published more than 150 titles, sold more than 150 million books, and been translated into more than 25 languages. But for one week a year, they're rock stars—artist-access-only, laminate-wearing, security-escorted rock stars with roadies and groupies." Its original members include celebrity literary names, such as Dave Barry, Tad Bartimus, Roy Blount Jr., Matt Groening, Josh Kelly, Stephen King, Barbara Kingsolver, Ridley Pearson, and others. With regard to its popularity, they proudly claim that they "have no music videos, no record contract, no Grammy nominations—but do have over 159,000 hits on Google" (http://www.rockbottomremainders.com/pages/history.html).

On November 6, 1991 after the exhausting book tour to promote *The Kitchen God's Wife*, Amy Tan received a fax message from Gold-mark asking her to join the newly formed rock band. Despite her initial hesitation to perform in public, Tan joined the group and became one of the original members simply "to have fun" (*Fate*, 153). Indeed, she enjoyed her experience. Tan debuted with the Rock Bottom Remainders at the 1992 American Booksellers Association convention in Anaheim, California. Thereafter, Tan has sung and performed with the band at a number of events across the United States. She has served as "lead rhythm dominatrix, backup singer, and second tambourine with the literary garage band" (http://amytan.net). Proceeds from their performances are donated to support literacy programs. Over the years, the Rock Bottom Remainders have raised over a million dollars. Singing in this band gives Tan an opportunity to reach back to the "proper politically incorrect mood" of her teenage years (*Fate,* 147). Writing fondly about her experience as a Remainder in *The Opposite of Fate,* she says that ultimately "the best part about being a Remainder was the fact that we became a family. We had family fun.... Our life together included getting neck cramps while sleeping on the bus, waking up and seeing how haggard we looked without coffee, without makeup" (*Fate,* 150). Videos of some of the Rock Bottom Remainders' performances are available on YouTube; for example, Amy Tan and her husband Louis DeMattei performing "Leader of the Pack" with the band at the 2006 Festival of Books at University of California at Los Angeles and Tan singing "It's My Party."

DISCUSSION QUESTIONS

- How does Tan incorporate popular culture into her writing? Find specific examples from her novels and explain how popular culture affects her writing, and in turn how her writing influences American popular culture.
- After reading *The Opposite of Fate,* discuss Amy Tan's attitude about the decline of reading books among contemporary Americans in a culture dominated by visual materials and the Internet.
- Analyze Amy Tan's unique language style and discuss how it relates to her fame in popular culture.
- Discuss Amy Tan's role as a children's literature writer and address the differences and similarities between her works for adults and her writing for children.

11

AMY TAN ON THE INTERNET

Since Amy Tan published her first book, *The Joy Luck Club,* almost two decades ago, the Internet has entered many people's lives in meaningful ways. It is not surprising that a famous writer like Tan would become a frequent name on the World Wide Web. A search of "Amy Tan" on Google on July 14, 2008 yielded 1,630,000 results. The Internet provides a variety of sources regarding Tan and her works. The vast amount of information available on the Internet undoubtedly expands her popularity, readership, and cultural influence, which further builds up her literary fame. Yet at the same time, this Internet barrage also incurs problematic side effects. For example, Tan has noted certain inaccurate facts about her being circulated on the Internet, starting with a few minor mistakes which then developed into widespread unbelievable errors. Tan's essay "Persona Errata," collected in *The Opposite of Fate,* addresses the epidemic inaccuracy on the Internet regarding her life and writing. She makes a list of Erratum 1 to 11 to correct the major errors she has found and promises to add to it regularly (*The Opposite of Fate,* 117-20). "Persona Errata" is also posted on Tan's personal Web site http://amytan.net/MythsAndLegends.aspx under the heading "Myths & Legends."

Selected Web Sites about Amy Tan

Amy Tan
http://amytan.net

Tan's home page includes a brief biography, events, links, photos, an essay on Lyme disease, and questions and answers about her novel *Saving Fish from Drowning*. There is a link to "Book Passage" where readers can order autographed copies, and another to the Steven Barclay Agency for lecture and other public appearance requests. In this sense, her site is also a marketing device for the author.

Tan's Web site not only provides information to readers and fans, but also shows what role the Internet has played in the author's personal life. In 2001, after returning from an exhausting four-month book tour to forty cities in the United States and another dozen overseas, Tan felt her body broken. Consulting both a psychiatrist and her regular doctor yet getting no confirmed diagnosis, Tan turned to the Internet. After going through multiple tests and ruling out many possible conditions, Tan reduced the list of candidates: multiple sclerosis, lupus, and Lyme disease. Various Web sites and pieces from her clouded memory led to Tan's conclusion that she was infected with Lyme disease from a tick a few years ago without noticing it. Tan's essay advises people to be aware of the disease and keep themselves informed about the symptoms and treatment.

The "Q & A" section of Tan's personal Web site addresses themes, characters, and other aspects of *Saving Fish from Drowning*. Responding to the question about whether this novel is a departure from her previous books, Tan states

> But up until then I had been writing about mothers and daughters because the beliefs I developed from my life with a difficult mother had occupied most of my thoughts. And I tend to write about the questions that continually haunt me. But my relationship with my mother toward the end of her life was wonderful, and usually writers write about what's not-so-wonderful. (http://amytan.net/InterviewWithAmyTan.aspx)

Tan also talks about the broader range of characters who are Caucasians and men featured in *Saving Fish from Drowning*: "My new book just brings into play more elements from my life, my multiple perspectives and interests" (http://amytan.net).

Red Room

http://www.redroom.com/author/amy-tan

Tan's home page links to this site for readers and authors where she maintains a page and started a blog in 2008. Her Red Room Writer Profile includes her biography, blogs, media, published works, reviews of her books, and events. The Web site also gives an opportunity for Internet surfers to write reviews of Tan's works. Under the section "Influences," Tan writes about different elements that have helped shape her life as well as her writing, for example the "Holy Ghost" of her father's Christian faith, the Chinese ghosts of her mother's beliefs, and the American Dream and the Chinese family's interpretation of it. The media section includes videos of Amy Tan giving talks, including "Amy Tan on Homeland Security," "Where Creativity Hides," "Amy Tan Talks about Music," and "Amy Tan Reads from *Saving Fish from Drowning*." Under "Events" Tan lists the San Francisco Opera performance of *The Bonesetter's Daughter*.

Academy of Achievement: A Museum of Living History

http://www.achievement.org/autodoc/page/tan0gal-1

The Academy of Achievement is a nonprofit established in 1961 in Washington D.C. to bring students into closer contact with today's leading thinkers and achievers. Its Web site inducted a page for Amy Tan in 1996, calling her "a uniquely personal storyteller." It includes the author's profile and biography, both of which were last updated in 2005. The photo gallery provides photos of Tan and her family and friends up to January 2008. The "Interview" section posts the full text of an interview with Tan that was conducted on June 28, 1996 in Sun Valley, Idaho. It also includes access to the video and audio clips to this interview. In addition, the navigation bar includes links to related Web sites, videos, and other relevant resources that would help teachers to prepare lesson plans featuring Tan using Achievement Curriculum materials. This Web site provides useful and up-to-date information to educators and readers.

Voices from the Gaps: Women Artists and Writers of Color, An International Website

http://voices.cla.umn.edu/vg/Bios/entries/tan_amy.html#trans

As stated on its home page, Voices from the Gaps is "a web-based trans-national academic community including students, teachers, artists, and scholars." This international Web site "provides resources about artists and writers," "forges a collective effort of scholars who digitally interact with each other," "contains biographical and critical analysis, pedagogical information, and histories of translation," and "archives recorded sound, film, and image collections, interviews, and online conversations with web logs (blogs)." Housed in the English Department at University of Minnesota, this site's page for Amy Tan was researched and submitted by Ted J. Sonquist on December 6, 1996, as part of his coursework for a Literature of American Minorities class at the University of Minnesota. It includes a brief biography of the author, criticism, works by and about the author, and related links. This Web site provides useful sources regarding Tan, yet it contains relatively limited information and has not been updated since 1996.

The Book Report Network

Established in 1996, the Book Report Network comprises Bookreporter. com, AuthorsOnTheWeb, AuthorYellowPages, FaithfulReader.com, ReadingGroupGuides.com, Teenreads.com, and Kidsreads.com. It provides "thoughtful book reviews, compelling features, in-depth author profiles and interviews, excerpts of the hottest new releases, literary games and contests, and more every week." Amy Tan's profile on Bookreporter.com (http://www. bookreporter.com/authors/au-tan-amy.asp) includes the author's bio, transcript of her talk on *Saving Fish from Drowning* in November 2005, and her interview with Bookreporter.com writer Jami Edwards in March 2001, in which she talked about her life, writing career, and *The Bonesetter's Daughter*. This Web site also includes links to reviews of *The Bonesetter's Daughter* and *Saving Fish from Drowning*, and to a reading group guide for *The Bonesetter's Daughter*. This page confirms the overall mission of the Book Report Network and places more emphasis on reviews and interviews of Tan's works than on information about her life and writing career.

SELECTED WEB SITES ABOUT *THE JOY LUCK CLUB*

Since *The Joy Luck Club* is not only a best seller but also a frequent title on many instructors' reading lists, resources of many kinds about this novel flourish on the Internet. Penguin Reading Guides (http://us. penguingroup.com/static/rguides/us/joy_luck_club.html), for example, include an introduction to the novel, a conversation with Amy Tan, and discussion questions for general readers. Lilia Melani's course page for "Core Studies 6: Landmarks of Literature," an English class offered at Brooklyn College in 2005, is another good example of Web sources for teaching *The Joy Luck Club*: http://academic.brooklyn.cuny.edu/english/melani/cs6/tan.html. Melani's Web page not only provides an overview of the author and the book and introduces the main themes and imagery, but also includes detailed guides and discussion questions for reading Tan's novel in three parts as well as links to other resources. Melani's course page is very useful for students and other readers to gain a comprehensive understanding of *The Joy Luck Club* within its social, cultural, and literary contexts. It contains helpful resources for instructors who utilize *The Joy Luck Club* in their classes.

Vocabulary Classic Texts (http://www.vocabulary.com/VUctjoyluck. html) has selected seventy-five words from *The Joy Luck Club* for students to study "SAT-College Prep vocabulary" in the context of a literary work. In her introduction, Etta Molly Gee, Professor of Library Science at Vocabulary University, explains that at the Classic Texts Web site "vocabulary has been pulled from many recommended texts" and her suggestions include: first of all, "individually or as a group, choose words that are unknown to you from the list. To help memorize, look up and write down the definition, part of speech and use the new word in a sentence of more than 6 words"; secondly, "write a story, postcard, letter or journal entry using 15–25 words in context"; and then "working individually or in a group, pair synonyms and/or antonyms. Determine how many words are adjectives, nouns and verbs." She reminds the reader that "vocabulary mastery comes from encountering new words in assigned reading, in studying vocabulary word lists and using words in context." According to the credit line included on the Web page, Janice Cook, a former teacher at Sacred Heart Prep in Atherton, California, served as the teacher contributor for *The Joy Luck Club* unit.

Established in 2000, Web English Teacher presents K-12 English and language arts teaching resources: lesson plans, WebQuests, videos, biography, e-texts, criticism, jokes, puzzles, and other classroom activities. This site helps educators use cyberspace to share ideas and resources and to find guidance and inspiration from one another. Web English Teacher provides lesson plans for teaching *The Joy Luck Club* and other works by Amy Tan, including an overview of the author with extensive analyses of her writing and themes, study guides, reading activities, commentaries, and discussion questions of Tan's *The Joy Luck Club*, *The Bonesetter's Daughter*, and *The Opposite of Fate* (http://www.webenglishteacher.com/tan.html). This Web page also contains lesson plans and classroom activities for the author's short stories "Rules of the Game" and "Two Kinds" as well as about her essay "Mother Tongue."

Founded by Cliff Hillegass with the prompting of Jack Cole, owner of Canada's Coles Notes, CliffsNotes, Inc. took shape in 1958. Since then it has published study guides in a number of disciplines, including literature, foreign languages, math, sciences, and other subjects. Now all the CliffsNotes literature guides are available free online, including its detailed study guide on *The Joy Luck Club* (http://www.cliffsnotes.com/WileyCDA/LitNote/The-Joy-Luck-Club.id-39.html). "About the Author" includes Amy Tan's profile; "About the Novel" contains an introduction to the *The Joy Luck Club* and a list of characters; "Summaries and Commentaries" provides detailed reading guides to each chapter; "Critical Essays" includes three essays on different topics; "Study Help" includes essay topics, review questions, and a quiz.

A similarly comprehensive study guide to *The Joy Luck Club* found at SparkNotes (http://sparknotes.com/lit/joyluck) features a user-friendly navigation drop-down menu for its all-encompassing content regarding Tan's novel, including context, plot overview, character list, analysis of major characters, themes, motifs and symbols, important quotations explained, key facts, study questions and essay topics, quiz, and suggestions for further reading. Printable SparkNotes on Tan's novel are available in a PDF file for a fee.

Another such Internet source is the study guide provided by eNotes at http://www.enotes.com/joy-luck, where information regarding Tan's novel can be viewed and downloaded in html and PDF formats for a membership fee or a one-time charge. It also contains a link to *The Joy Luck Club Lesson Plan* where teachers can purchase different lesson plans in downloadable PDF files. Another example is the free online study guide, notes, and summary of *The Joy Luck Club* at The Best Notes: http://thebestnotes.com/booknotes/Joy_Luck_Club_Tan/Joy_Luck_Club_Study_Guide01.html, last updated on May 13, 2008.

For a subscription fee, Teach With Movies provides teachers and parents with lesson plans and learning guides to 285 movies, among them the film adaptation of *The Joy Luck Club* (http://www.teachwith-movies.org/guides/joy-luck-club.html). The Web site states that "[e]ach film recommended by Teach With Movies contains lessons on life and positive moral messages. Our Guides and Lesson Plans show teachers and parents how to stress these messages and make them meaningful for your audiences."

Selected Web Sites about *The Kitchen God's Wife*

Answers.com provides a detailed study guide to *The Kitchen God's Wife* (http://www.answers.com/topic/the-kitchen-god-s-wife) including the author's biography, plot summary, characters, themes, style, historical context, critical overview, criticism, questions, sources, and further reading. SparkNotes provides more comprehensive learning guides to this novel (http://

sparknotes.com/lit/kitchengods), including an online quiz as well as discussion and essay topics. Printable SparkNotes on Tan's novel are available in a PDF file for a fee. eNotes provides a study guide to *The Kitchen God's Wife* in printable and PDF formats with a fee for membership or a one-time charge (http://www.enotes.com/kitchen-gods). Another comprehensive source is offered by BookRags.com (http://www.bookrags.com/The_Kitchen_God's_Wife) where readers can print out or download the 169-page study guide to Tan's novel for a fee.

Bella Adams's brief overview of *The Kitchen God's Wife* was published in *The Literary Encyclopedia* online on November 8, 2002 (http://litencyc.com/php/sworks.php?rec=true&UID=440). Some other book reviews of *The Kitchen God's Wife* are available online, such as Holly Smith's review in *500 Great Books by Women* (http://www.tuvy.com/resource/books/k/Kitchen_Gods_Wife.html) and Wendy Smith's review (http://www.cheneysmith.com/wen/kitchen.htm).

OTHER INTERNET RESOURCES

Amy Tan's popularity as a contemporary writer is certainly reflected on the Internet. Among the fan sites, Anniina's Amy Tan Page (http://www.luminarium.org/contemporary/amytan) is a good example. This Web site compiles useful resources about the author such as a brief biographical note and a bibliography of her work, plus links to official sites, biographical sites, interviews, bibliographical information, miscellaneous, book reviews and study resources organized by book title. First created on February 21, 1996 by Anniina Jokinen, this site was last updated in October 2007.

On YouTube.com, readers can find videos of Tan and her husband performing with The Rock Bottom Remainders. There are also video clips of Tan's book readings and interviews available on YouTube.

DISCUSSION QUESTIONS

- Carefully review two Web sites that provide biographical and bibliographical information about Tan and compare their correctness regarding the author and her works.
- Carefully review two Web sites that provide study guides to *The Joy Luck Club* and compare their usefulness for studying the text.

- Carefully review two Web sites that provide study guides to *The Kitchen God's Wife* and compare their usefulness for studying the text.
- Discuss the pros and cons of the Internet study guides (for example, CliffsNotes) to Tan's works, especially *The Joy Luck Club*. To what extent are they beneficial for readers and students and to what extent are they not?
- Search for a fan site related to Amy Tan and review the author's official home page at http://amytan.net. Comment on the fan site's correctness and appropriateness.
- Read Tan's essay "Persona Errata" available at http://amytan.net/Myths AndLegends.aspx, and discuss the positive and negative effects of the Internet in regard to Tan's life and writing career.
- Review Tan's official website, http://amytan.net, and discuss how she uses the Internet to promote her works.

12

AMY TAN AND THE MEDIA

A reviewer for the *Telegraph*, a British newspaper Web site, writes: "Tan refers to herself several times as a 'literary writer,' but she is that rare phenomenon, a writer whose success has earned her a place in the broader culture: televised, filmed, interviewed, reported on, she is insofar as any literary figure in America can be, a celebrity" (Messud 2003). Indeed, as one of the most popular writers of contemporary American literature, Amy Tan, together with her works, have caught a plethora of attention from the media in book reviews, interviews, television appearances, and news articles.

RECEPTION OF *THE JOY LUCK CLUB*

Tan's acclaimed debut book, *The Joy Luck Club*, won a number of awards and nominations. It was chosen to be one of the American Library Association's Notable Books and selected for the National Endowment for the Arts 2007 Big Read program. Reviews of *The Joy Luck Club* were overwhelmingly positive. Different reviewers highly praised Tan's clear yet sophisticated writing style, thematic complexity, intricate mother-daughter relationships portrayed in a multifaceted narrative structure, comprehensive portrayals of Chinese American characters' identity struggles, and the universal appeal to readers of various backgrounds. For example, Scarlet Cheng's review published in *Belles Lettres* shortly after the release of *The Joy Luck Club* paid tribute to its

On Amy Tan's personal Web page, http://amytan.net, her interview addresses various aspects of her most recent publication, *Saving Fish from Drowning*. In her responses to the interview questions, Tan talks about her newest novel's departure from her previous works such as a focus on the present rather than the past, a change of subject from the family relationships to romances and adventures, a group of non-Asian characters, a setting in Burma, and the political implications within a "comic novel." In particular, Tan talks about the power of media, especially the issues of television and reality shows, that make up an important theme of her novel. In a media-dominant era, according to Tan, fiction's importance and relevance among readers are more than ever since "imagination is the closest thing we have to compassion. To have compassion you have to be able to imagine the lives of others. . . . Fiction has a huge role in presenting the truth of anything—not the facts, but the feelings, what you feel, what others feel, what your moral position is, your version of truth" (http://amytan.net). In *Saving Fish from Drowning*, Tan writes about how the media shape the news and affect reality, especially during the search for the American tourists in Burma. "In the novel, the good part is that the media help the travelers get saved. The bad part is that Harry is in collusion with the junta and more tourists come to visit a country that is supposed to be boycotted" (http://amytan.net). The complexity embedded in her fiction leads the reader to review the media in modern society.

"clarity of voice and lucidity of vision" that "reveals to us that for all life's contradictions and tragedies, the true path of existence is convergence" (Cheng 1989, 12). Commending Tan's successful handling of complex themes, Orville Schell's review for the *New York Times* read

> In the hands of a less talented writer such thematic material might easily have become overly didactic, and the characters might have seemed like cutouts from a Chinese-American knockoff of "Roots." But in the hands of Amy Tan, who has a wonderful eye for what is telling, a fine ear for dialogue, a deep empathy for her subject matter and a guilelessly straightforward way of writing, they sing with a rare fidelity and beauty. She has written a jewel of a book. (Schell, 28)

With regard to the mother-daughter relationships, Scarlet Cheng's review for *Belles Lettres* focused on language and cultural differences: "The two languages are literal, as well as figurative, because even in English the mothers speak with the cadence and the mindset of the Chinese. While they frequently mangle idioms … these inadvertent neologisms are uncannily apt, as are the mothers' twisted observations of American life" (Cheng 1989, 12). Similarly, Merle Rubin's review for the *Christian Science Monitor* stated: "The daughters' difficulty in comprehending their mothers is echoed by the mothers' frustration at not being able to pass on the benefits of their accumulated wisdom and experience" (Rubin, 13). Rubin's review also praised the remarkable narration of Tan's novel and considers *The Joy Luck Club* "a touching, funny, sad, insightful, and artfully constructed group portrait of four mother-daughter relationships that endure not only a generation gap, but the more unbridgeable gap between two cultures" (Rubin, 13). Cheng and Rubin's positive remarks on Tan's intertwined portrayal of the generational differences and connections reflect the views of many critics and readers.

John Skow's review for *Time* magazine situated Tan's novel within the context of Chinese American literature and by extension Asian American literature. Skow stated: "Amy Tan's bright, sharp-flavored first novel belongs on a short shelf dominated by Maxine Hong Kingston's remarkable works of a decade or so ago, *The Woman Warrior* and *China Men*" (Skow, 98). Considering Tan's bicultural heritage, Skow claimed that she "writes with both inside and outside knowing, and her novel rings clearly, like a fine porcelain bowl" (Skow, 98). In this sense, *The Joy Luck Club* helped expand the media's interest as well as that of the general public in Asian American literature.

Conducted three weeks before the publication of *The Joy Luck Club*, interviewer Katherine Usher Henderson described Tan's comfortable living room as "surrounded by tangible artifacts of Tan's Chinese heritage" and the writer herself as "soft-spoken but articulate; she laughs frequently, both at herself and at some of the lighter ironies that have marked her life" (Henderson, 15). Henderson praised Tan's ability to keep a balance between her two cultural heritages and included many biographical facts about Tan in the interview:

> Through writing, remembering, and renewed contact with Chinese culture, Tan has come to understand both sides of her heritage and the sometimes comic, sometimes tragic tensions between them. Her rich heritage, her brilliance, her total commitment to fiction, and the unique power of her imagination … make her a writer of great vision and even greater promise. (Henderson, 21–22)

Henderson's prophecy has proven to be right. "Talking about mother-daughter relationships in general, Tan referred to 'the metaphor of the umbilical cord … which gets stretched over time; whether it's the mother or daughter who severs it or tries to pull it tighter, part of that is individual and part is cultural'" (Henderson, 16). Like many immigrant children, although Tan tried to assimilate thoroughly when she was young, "she was in fact storing up memories, including stories her mother told her about her grandparents that would lead her eventually to *The Joy Luck Club*" (Henderson, 17). The writing process is her way of paying tribute to her mother and her bicultural heritage.

Donna Seaman's interview for *Booklist* magazine focused more on writing, literature, and a writer's role. Seaman spoke with Tan at the 1990 American Literature Association Annual Conference in Chicago where Tan was the featured speaker at the RASD/Notable Books Council Breakfast. When asked to address the truths in *The Joy Luck Club*, Tan responded, "All the emotions are definitely true" (Seaman). While talking about the clear and pure prose style, Tan said

> I really was writing *The Joy Luck Club* for my mother. And I thought, here's this intelligent person, and I want to write for her in a way that the emotions come through and the story comes through and the words are never more important than the story. I wanted to convey images through the language, and I believe that you can do this in a way that is very clear and accessible to the reader. As for the writer's ego, you try to let go of that as much as possible. (Seaman)

When addressing childhood imagination and a writer's life, Tan remarked: "Childhood is a time of really trying to make sense of so many things. You're learning so much, learning who you should pay attention to, learning what's real in the world and what's imaginary. I remember so much of my childhood as being confused, not knowing if things were in my imagination or really as I saw them" (Seaman). This interview, similar to many others, addresses the connection between Tan's life and writing career.

RECEPTION OF *THE KITCHEN GOD'S WIFE*

Despite the myth of the "doomed" second book, *The Kitchen God's Wife* achieved huge success. *The Kitchen God's Wife* was a *New York Times* Notable Book, an American Library Association Notable Book, and a Booklist Editors' Choice. Elgy Gillespie's review for the *San Francisco Review of Books* spoke for many critics and readers:

> It is indeed possible to pull off a second novel as good as (and perhaps better than) the first. It is also quite possible for a best-

seller to be an estimable piece of writing as well as a ripping read, something I only came to credit quite recently. Once again I found myself reading Amy Tan all night, unable to put the story down until I knew what happened in the end, sniffling when I got to the sad bits (specially the loss of Yiku and Danru, Winnie's first babies) and finally going to sleep at dawn with the conviction that Tan had provided an education for the heart. (Gillespie, 33–34)

Rave reviews began appearing shortly after its publication: "A ravishing, vivid, graceful, and unforgettable tale of womanhood, endurance and love, lit by gentle humor and the healing aspect of truth. Stock up. Amy Tan's admirers are growing into a voracious legion," said the reviewer for the *American Librarian* (Gillespie, 33–34). Some reviewers looked at Tan's equally successful second novel as a confirmation of the author's literary talent and her position in contemporary American literature. Helen Yglesias's review for the *Women's Review of Books*, for example, remarked

Amy Tan commands an intriguing style which, along with her highly special subject matter, makes for a unique contribution to contemporary writing. *The Joy Luck Club* introduced her as a young novelist; more or less inevitably, what she had to say was not entirely successfully done the first time. It is to our advantage that she returned to her powerful material for another try. (Yglesias, 1, 3)

Newsweek called it "the kind of novel that can be read and reread with enormous pleasure" (http://www.tuvy.com/resource/books/k/Kitchen_ Gods_Wife.html). With another engaging narrative, Tan proved herself to be a unique storyteller "gifted with a quirky style, a broad historical sense, and great energy" (Yglesias, 1, 3).

A number of book reviews addressed *The Kitchen God's Wife* in comparison with *The Joy Luck Club*. Helen Yglesias's review pointed to the strength of Tan's writing in multiple ways: narrating the story in an intricate structure, weaving "trivia into rich and illuminating character portrayal," and evoking "large positive emotions without descending into sentimentality," all of which might make *The Kitchen God's Wife* surpass *The Joy Luck Club*. Comparing it to *The Joy Luck Club*, Robb Forman Dew stated that Tan's fans will not be disappointed by *The Kitchen God's Wife,* a "more ambitious effort and, in the end, greatly satisfying" (Dew, 9). Similar to *The Joy Luck Club, The Kitchen God's*

Wife "enfolds the dreams, tales, and lives of the Chinese mother and her Chinese-American daughter. But this time, instead of listening to multiple stories, we hear only two, and then only one—the wife's tale" (Wendy Smith). Instead of the "multiple micronarrative approach" she used in writing *The Joy Luck Club*, Tan focuses on the relationship between one mother-daughter pair in the tradition of "matrilineal literature" (Adams, "*The Kitchen God's Wife*"). Elgy Gillespie considered *The Kitchen God's Wife* "a more satisfying book than its predecessor" (Gillespie, 33–34) because Tan's second novel deals with similar themes in more profound and sensitive ways, and its narrative structure unfolds truths gradually as the story progresses.

With regard to the portrayal of the characters, Tan's second novel creates a comic and at the same time sorrowful effect: "What gives *The Kitchen God's Wife* its distinction is the refreshingly sweet-sour and practical attitude of the older generation" (Fitzgerald, 19). Taking on her mother's voice and the voice of that generation, "Tan displays superb storytelling—spinning personae and situations that are credible and compelling. But more, she has the courage to share heartfelt sorrow and grief, to acknowledge human imperfection and fate's ambiguities" (Cheng 1991, 19). In this sense, Winnie's story is a personal saga as well as a narrative for women of her generation. "Almost every page of the old wife's tale is lit up with the everyday magic of a world in which birds can sound like women crying and sweaters are knit in the memory of spider webs. Yet all the storybook marvels are grounded in a survivor's vinegar wit" (Iyer). At the end of the novel, forgiveness eventually bridges the gaps between generations.

Critics and reviewers have addressed Tan's second novel as a book representing Chinese and Chinese American culture in particular as well as a work of contemporary American literature in general. Ceneta Lee Williams praised it as "[a] wonderful story, full of the richness of Chinese culture and language. Amy Tan really took me into her life, past and present. She has a great way of conveying the language and the images that only one from her world and experiences would know" (http://www.tuvy.com/resource/books/k/Kitchen_Gods_Wife.html). Part of the reason for Tan's appeal to a broad range of readers is her rich story of life that encompasses grief, imperfection, ambiguity, and triumph, "a triumph of the spirit, of the human soul to endure, to show compassion, and to hold fast to dreams" (Cheng 1991, 19). These universal themes are represented through her unique storytelling.

Besides the overwhelmingly positive reception of Tan's second novel, there were also critiques. Robb Forman Dew's review recognized the value of *The Kitchen God's Wife* but at the same time pointed out some flaws such as "a slow start," a seemingly stereotypical character of Winnie, and a sometimes awkward method as "the obstacle of the framework" (Dew, 9). Similarly, Ragini Venkatasubban addressed the thematic repetition in *The Kitchen God's Wife* and viewed it as another vehicle for the author to "continue lamenting the difficulties of her childhood and adolescence," and overall considered Tan's second book to be "a painful and emotionally draining novel about secrets that leaves the reader with mixed feelings" (Venkatasubban, 42).

RECEPTION OF *THE HUNDRED SECRET SENSES*

Many reviewers and readers have noted the thematic changes in Tan's third novel, *The Hundred Secret Senses*. In this book, Tan tells the story of two half sisters through venturing into the realm of spirits and reincarnation, in which "ghosts replace memories as the link between past and present" (Nurse, 85). A finalist for the Orange Prize, this book was not as successful as Tan's previous works, but was still well received. A captivating tale of the sisterly bond, *The Hundred Secret Senses* gradually "reveals a series of family secrets that question one's fate, beliefs, imagination and faith" (Kelsey, 49). Presenting an "effortless mix of invention and reliance on reality," Tan provides "what is most irresistible in popular fiction: a feeling of abundance, an account so circumstantial, powerful and ingenious that it seems the story could go on forever" (Mesic, 1, 11). Such remarks confirm that Tan's intriguing story appeals to many readers.

In particular, the character Kwan received plenty of attention from the media. A character of "saintly good humor with wit, practicality and guile" (Pavey, 38), Kwan is empowered by her *yin* eyes to serve as a medium to bridge different periods of time, geographical locations, and a series of events. Her dreams "comprise the most skillfully realized sections of the novel, mingling elements of gothic romance and folktale with historical chronicle" and "remote landscapes and lifetimes" (Nurse, 85). To some degree, Kwan is an ordinary woman, "unstylish, scarcely educated, a tireless advice-giver and boringly down to earth in her preoccupation with family, ailments and bargains," yet in other ways, she is a unique character with "uncanny abilities" (Mesic, 1, 11). She "is a memorable creation. Of her belief in the World of Yin there can be no doubt. She emerges as a character at once innocent and wise, the relative Olivia both suffers and relies upon. Kwan gently forces Olivia to face the worst in herself and, in so doing, to find her strengths. We could all do with such a sister" (Messud 1995, 11). Kwan adds a new image to Tan's literary collage of women characters.

Despite its mostly positive reception, *The Hundred Secret Senses* incurred criticism. For example, Claire Messud's review in the *New York Times Book Review* considered Tan's third novel "a mildly entertaining and slightly ridiculous ghost story" (Messud 1995, 11). Messud's comments voiced some readers and critics' disapproval of Tan's tale of reincarnation, spirit, and ghosts.

In an interview with Gretchen Giles, titled "Bay Area Author Amy Tan Talks about Fame and Phantoms," Tan talks about *The Hundred Secret Senses;* how her childhood, cultural heritage, and family affected her writing; and her experience of becoming a storyteller. Addressing her celebrity status that is not common for literary writers, Tan said

> I have a public persona, and what I do with it now *is* to have fun with it.... I used to resent feeling that I was giving away bits and pieces of myself—that my privacy was being invaded—but now I happily give away this part of my persona which is just the fun part. I used to dread the readings, and go home and gnash my teeth, and now I just do it and it's over. I forget it and I just go back to the non-persona, the private persona, which can be fun too. I don't take it seriously. I know that *that* name is out there. (Giles; italics in the original)

These words lay out Tan's general attitude toward media reception and the treatment of her and of her works as well as her interaction with the media as part of her public persona.

Reception of *The Opposite of Fate*

Tan's first book of nonfiction, *The Opposite of Fate,* was a *New York Times* Notable Book and a Booklist Editors' Choice. Its audio abridged version won the Audie Award for Best Nonfiction, Abridged. The subtitle, "a book of musings," accurately describes "the casual tone and seemingly random nature" of Tan's "patchwork memoir, a chronicle of Tan's fears and delusions, inner journeys and real-world struggles, roots of grief and sources of inspiration" (Beason). Reviews for this book were mixed. Praising the collection of essays, Deborah Mason, for example, complimented Tan's "excursions into past lives" and "cunning willfulness of memory" that helped to produce strong essays. Similar to her fiction, "Tan's nonfiction effortlessly blends dark and light, past and present, logical and magical" (Beason) and offers insight into the author's personal life and writing career. "Tan's thoughtful analysis of the people, places, choices and circumstances—the opposite of fate—in her life will make her fans appreciate her gifts even more" (Crow). *The Opposite of Fate* thus provides a helpful companion to Tan's fictional works. Moreover, some of the essays collected in *The Opposite of Fate* reflect the author's critical views of current issues. "Her refusal to be classified into an Asian American literary ghetto, for example, is proudly argued, as is her defense for both her mother's native language and the bilingual patois she grew up with" (Simon).

On the negative side, Claire Messud criticized Tan's book of nonfiction for failing to develop the source materials into a "moving and potentially significant" memoir; the author's thoughts reflected in *The Opposite of Fate* "are of no apparent interest" and detrimental to her essays (Messud 2003). In addition, Liz Hoggard's review published in the *Observer* in Britain gave overall positive comments on the book but pointed out some flaws including the uneven assembly of Tan's essays. It called *The Opposite of Fate* "a mixed bag. At times, the breezy, home-spun pieces … sit oddly with Tan's harrowing first-person testimony" (Hoggard). Jane Shilling also criticized Tan's nonfiction because of the variable quality of the fragments. She remarked: "But the regretting of unwritten books is a peculiarly hollow exercise. Besides, this collage or mosaic of bright shards has an immediacy and freshness of spirit that might have vanished from something more highly wrought" (Shilling).

Jay MacDonald's interview with Tan covered her collection *The Opposite of Fate*, her struggle with Lyme disease, and her involvement with the Rock Bottom Remainders band. Tan said: "I've only had one life and these are the aspects of my life that I continue to dwell upon.... We as writers, when we talk about what our oeuvre is, we go back to the same questions and the same pivotal moments in our lives and they become the themes in our writing" (MacDonald). MacDonald remarked: "*The Opposite of Fate* captures a life fully lived in 32 chapters, from Tan's award-winning essay at age 8 to her unlikely adolescence in Switzerland … to the ghost in her San Francisco condo … to the filming of *The Joy Luck Club*." His comments illustrate the broad coverage of Tan's book of nonfiction.

A 2003 interview with Tan titled "A Life Stranger than Fiction" made a close connection between the writer's colorful family background and life experience on the one hand and her writing on the other, as it addressed *The Opposite of Fate*. Describing Tan as speaking "in a soft voice with a West-Coast American accent," the interviewer shared that Tan "has an engaging giggle and is far more friendly than she sounds in her book" (de Bertodano). Vignettes like this help provide to the reader an image of the author.

ARTICLES AND INTERVIEWS RELATED TO AMY TAN AND HER WORKS

Not as influential as *The Joy Luck Club* or *The Kitchen God's Wife*, Tan's novel *The Bonesetter's Daughter* was nominated for the Orange Prize and the IMPAC Dublin Award, and was a *New York Times* Notable Book. Tan made an appearance on *Good Morning America* in 2001, in which she stated that *The Bonesetter's Daughter* was her "most personal publication" (Snodgrass, 25). Another interview of Tan about this book with Bill Thompson is available online at http://www.eyeonbooks. com/ibp.php?ISBN=0399146431.

Tan's novel *Saving Fish from Drowning* was nominated for the IMPAC Dublin Award and was a Booklist Editors' Choice, yet still received mixed reviews. A reviewer for the *Independent*, Lisa Gee, praised Tan's "cute opening device" and the "engaging and enjoyable" story line, yet criticized her failing the "ambitious task" of portraying thirteen protagonists as well as a group of supporting characters, which is too much "to keep in mind whilst reading." Carol Memmott's review for *USA Today* took a positive tone and complimented the novel as "a hilarious yet politically charged tale packed with illusions and the human capacity for love." Through her group portrait of the characters, Tan lays out a picture of "humankind's foibles: the lovelorn, the infertile, the sex-starved, the hypochondriacs, the arrogant, the insecure, the paranoid and the self-absorbed" (Memmott). Andrew Solomon's review for the *New York Times* emphasized Tan's success in filling a sophisticated adventure story with humor, irony, evocative images, and charming landscape, but at the same time pointed out the cliché-ridden characters, the patronizing attitude toward the Karen people, and the manipulative aspect of the book's setup. Solomon concluded that "Amy Tan is wonderful at old fictions of ancient lands; let us hope she will return to that territory in the future" (Solomon, 22).

Besides speaking all over the country and internationally at book signings, invited lectures, and other events, Tan also has appeared frequently on radio and television programs. On October 19, 2005, Tan talked with *Today* show host Katie Couric about *Saving Fish from Drowning*. Readers can watch the interview and read excerpts of the novel at http://www. msnbc.msn.com/id/9742414.

On December 5, 2005, Tan talked to Lisa Allardice from the *Guardian* about luck, a writer's life, and her novel *Saving Fish from Drowning*.

Titled "All about her mother," this interview began with Tan's anecdote about a dinner at the British Embassy in Washington where Margaret Thatcher mistook Tan for Jung Chang, author of *Wild Swans* (1981), before moving on to address Tan's resented tag of "writer of colour." The review remarked: "[w]hile *Saving Fish from Drowning* is as engaging and sparky as ever, Tan fans may be disappointed not to find the heart-tugging narratives they have come to expect." The interview concluded with a positive message from Tan that she would continue to write her "best book" with each book that she writes (Allardice).

A 1996 interview with Tan titled "A Uniquely Personal Storyteller" is posted on the Academy of Achievement Web site, including a full transcript as well as video and audio clips. Tan talked about her childhood, imagination, language, and writing. Tan once again emphasizes the importance of books in her life. "Reading for me was a refuge. I could escape from everything that was miserable in my life and I could be anyone I wanted to be in a story, through a character." Furthermore, she addresses the storytelling tradition in her family. "There was a lot of storytelling going on in our house: family stories, gossip, what happened to the people left behind in China." As a result of parental pressure for academic success and the harassment from a young minister when she was a teenager, Tan became "a very strong advocate for freedom of speech, freedom of expression, and the danger of banning books. The danger is in creating the idea that somebody else is going to define the purpose of literature and confine who has access to it" (http://www. achievement.org/autodoc/page/tan0int-1). This advocacy is particularly prominent in *Saving Fish from Drowning*.

Donna Longenecker's news report published in the *UB Reporter* in 2003 recounts Tan's talk as part of the University at Buffalo's Distinguished Speakers Series in the Center for the Arts Mainstage Theatre on March 26, 2003. In her speech, Tan reflected upon her childhood, her relationships with her parents, and how her life experience has influenced her writing career. Longenecker concludes her report by citing Tan's assertion that she needs a narrative to surround the chaos in her life and put it into order.

In the video *Changing Lanes*, Tan is among the renowned people in the arts, public service, and the sciences who discuss with students how they changed lanes unexpectedly in their career paths. Also featured are Douglas G. Carlston, Charles Kuralt, Dr. Nathan P. Myhrvold, Dr. Antonia C. Novello, and Martha Stewart (http://www.achievement.org/autodoc/giftshop/detail/atv031).

Tan is also a frequent guest on radio and television shows. A search for "Amy Tan" on the National Public Radio (NPR) Web site leads to more than thirty results, in which Tan talks on "All Things Considered," "Weekend Edition," and other programs about her books, China, and other topics. Audio clips on NPR's Web site, for example, include Tan's talks with Liane Hansen, Scott Simon, Robert Siegel, and others (http:// www.npr.org).

As part of the BBC series *Belief*, a transcript of an interview with Amy Tan at her New York home is available on BBC's Web site, in which she talks about belief and religion, and how they affected her family and her life. Readers can find a number of audio clips on this Web site in which she talks about her books on different programs such as on the "Woman's Hour," "BBC News Channel," "The Verb," and "World Book Club" (http://www.bbc.co.uk).

In addition, video and audio clips of Tan's readings, speeches, and interviews can be found on the Web at FORA.tv (http://fora.tv/fora/ showthread.php?t=444), Academy of Achievement (http://www.achieve-ment.org/autodoc/page/tan0int-1), and Wired for Books (http://wiredfor-books.org/amytan/). She also has made appearances in a number of videos, such as *Writing Women's Lives*, originally produced for televi-sion in 1995 and now available on DVD.

DISCUSSION QUESTIONS

- Watch one of the interviews with Tan available online and discuss how she uses the media to address her life and writing career as well as to promote her works.
- Compare two reviews of one of Tan's books and discuss how the media have treated the author and her works.
- After reading *Saving Fish from Drowning*, discuss how Tan writes about the role and influence of the media in contemporary life in her fiction.

13

WHAT DO I READ NEXT?

Reading works by women writers has intrigued Amy Tan's interest in fiction writing. The female sensibility found in these works has profoundly influenced her writing career. Those interested in Tan's fiction may also like to read the following works by women writers:

Beautiful Girl (stories) and *Almost Perfect* by Alice Adams

The House of the Spirits and *Of Love and Shadows* by Isabel Allende

The Lone Pilgrim (stories), *Family Happiness*, and *Another Marvelous Thing* by Laurie Colwin

Stones for Ibarra and *Under an Aztec Sun* (stories) by Harriet Doerr

Jacklight (poems), *Love Medicine*, *The Beet Queen*, and *Tracks* by Louise Erdrich

Rough Translations (stories) and *Creek Walk and Other Stories* by Molly Giles

Reasons to Live (stories), *At the Gates of the Animal Kingdom* (stories), and *Tumble Home: A Novella and Short Stories* by Amy Hempel

Anagrams and *Like Life* (stories) by Lorrie Moore

Dance of the Happy Shades (stories), *Lives of Girls and Women*, and *Something I've Been Meaning to Tell You: Thirteen Stories* by Alice Munro

A Good Man Is Hard to Find and Other Stories and *The Violent Bear It Away* by Flannery O'Connor

The Tin Can Tree and *Morgan's Passing* by Anne Tyler
In Love & Trouble: Stories of Black Women, You Can't Keep a Good Woman Down (stories), and *The Color Purple* by Alice Walker
The Golden Apples (stories) and *The Wide Net and Other Stories* by Eudora Welty

Most of Tan's novels feature women characters. For example, *The Joy Luck Club* focuses on women's lives and is told in women's voices. This narrative strategy is carried on in *The Kitchen God's Wife*, *The Hundred Secret Senses*, and *The Bonesetter's Daughter*. Readers who are interested in women's stories and feminist perspective may find the following works worthwhile reading:

Making Waves: An Anthology of Writings by and about Asian American Women edited by Asian Women United of California
The House of the Prophet by Louis Auchincloss
Asian-American Women Writers edited by Harold Bloom
Feminism in Literature: A Gale Critical Companion edited by Jessica Bomarito, Jeffrey Hunter, and Amy Hudock
Learning from My Mother's Voice: Family Legend and the Chinese American Experience by Jean Lau Chin
Filthy Fictions: Asian American Literature by Women by Monica Chiu
Leaving Deep Waters: Asian American Women at the Crossroads of Two Cultures by Claire S. Chow
Assimilating Asians: Gendered Strategies of Authorship in Asian America by Patricia P. Chu
The House on Mango Street by Sandra Cisneros
The Broom Closet: Secret Meanings of Domesticity in Postfeminist Novels by Louise Erdrich, Mary Gordon, Toni Morrison, Marge Piercy, Jane Smiley, and Amy Tan by Jeannette Batz Cooperman
The Aguero Sisters by Cristina García
Images of Asian American Women by Asian American Women Writers by Esther Mikyung Ghymn
A Virtuous Woman by Kaye Gibbons
The Other Side by Mary Gordon
Negotiating Identities: An Introduction to Asian American Women's Writing by Helena Grice
Making More Waves: New Writing by Asian American Women edited by Elaine H. Kim, Lilia Villanueva, and Asian Women United of California
The Americas of Asian American Literature: Gendered Fictions of Nation and Transnation by Rachel C. Lee

Between Worlds: Women Writers of Chinese Ancestry by Amy
  Ling
*New Visions of Community in Contemporary American Fiction:
  Tan, Kingsolver, Castillo, Morrison* by Magali Cornier Michael
Beloved and *Sula* by Toni Morrison
Inter/View: Talks with America's Writing Women by Mickey
  Pearlman and Katherine Usher Henderson
Stone, Paper, Knife by Marge Piercy
*Transnational, National, and Personal Voices: New Perspectives on
  Asian American and Asian Diasporic Women Writers* edited by
  Begoña Simal and Elisabetta Marino
A Thousand Acres by Jane Smiley
Women of Color in U.S. Society edited by Maxine Baca Zinn and
  Bonnie Thornton Dill

Tan entered the literary world with her compelling stories of mothers
and daughters in *The Joy Luck Club*. Her exploration of the complex
bonds and conflicts between the two generations appeals to many readers regardless of their cultural background. Those who take pleasure in
reading Tan's stories of mother-daughter relationships might find the following works interesting:

*Women of Color: Mother-Daughter Relationships in 20th-Century
  Literature* by Elizabeth Brown-Guillory
The Mother/Daughter Plot: Narrative, Psychoanalysis, Feminism
  by Marianne Hirsch
*In Her Mother's House: The Politics of Asian American Mother-
  Daughter Writing* by Wendy Ho

Tan's writing, particularly *The Joy Luck Club*, has attracted young
adult readers due to its accessible language style as well as stories of generational relationships. Those who are interested in the coming-of-age
theme in Tan's books may also enjoy other literary works for young
adults such as

Nice Girl from Good Home by Fran Arrick
Amazing Gracie by A. E. Cannon
Echoes of the White Giraffe by Sook Nyul Choi
Taking the Ferry Home by Pam Conrad
*Begin Here: Reading Asian North American Autobiographies of
  Childhood* by Rocío G. Davis
Pick-Up Sticks by Sarah Ellis
Growing up Asian American: An Anthology edited by Maria Hong

Farewell to Manzanar by Jeanne Wakatsuki Houston and James
    Houston
Obasan by Joy Kogawa

Most of Tan's works feature Chinese and Chinese American characters coping with their experiences in China and the United States.
Because of her popularity, Tan plays an important role in helping shape
contemporary American readers' perception of Chinese and Chinese
Americans. Those interested in Chinese American novels and memoirs
might want to read

*The Big Aiiieeeee!: An Anthology of Chinese American and
    Japanese American Literature* edited by Jeffery Paul Chan, Frank
    Chin, Lawson Fusao Inada, and Shawn Wong
Bound Feet & Western Dress by Pang-Mei Natasha Chang
Donald Duk and *The Chinaman Pacific & Frisco R.R. Co.* by
    Frank Chin
Paper Son: One Man's Story by Tung Pok Chin with Winifred C. Chin
Eat a Bowl of Tea by Louis Chu
Typical American, *Mona in the Promised Land*, *Who's Irish?*
    (stories), and *The Love Wife* by Gish Jen
Waiting, *War Trash*, *The Bridegroom* (stories), and *Under the Red
    Flag* (stories) by Ha Jin
The Woman Warrior: Memoirs of a Girlhood among Ghosts,
    China Men and *Tripmaster Monkey: His Fake Book* by Maxine
    Hong Kingston
The Flower Drum Song by C. Y. Lee
China Boy and *Chasing Hepburn: A Memoir of Shanghai,
    Hollywood, and a Chinese Family's Fight for Freedom* by Gus
    Lee
Paper Daughter by M. Elaine Mar
Red Azalea, *Becoming Madame Mao*, and *Katherine* by Anchee Min
Bone and *Steer Toward Rock* by Fae Myenne Ng
Eating Chinese Food Naked by Mei Ng
*On Gold Mountain: The One-Hundred-Year Odyssey of My
    Chinese-American Family*, *Snow Flower and the Secret Fan*, and
    Peony in Love by Lisa See
Fifth Chinese Daughter by Jade Snow Wong
Homebase and *American Knees* by Shawn Wong

In her fiction, the personal stories of Tan's characters are often interwoven with their historical, social, and cultural contexts. In this sense,
fiction, history, and memory are blended together. Readers who are

interested in learning more about Asian American history, experiences, and culture which informs Tan's writing may want to read

> *Race, Rights, and the Asian American Experience* by Angelo N. Ancheta
>
> *Asian Americans: An Interpretive History* and *Remapping Asian American History* by Sucheng Chan
>
> *The Rape of Nanking: The Forgotten Holocaust of World War II* by Iris Chang
>
> *An Interethnic Companion to Asian American Literature* edited by King-Kok Cheung
>
> *Lives of Notable Asian Americans: Literature and Education* by Christina Chiu
>
> *Asian/Pacific Islander American Women: A Historical Anthology* edited by Shirley Hune and Gail M. Nomura
>
> *Asian American Literature: An Introduction to the Writings and Their Social Context* by Elaine H. Kim
>
> *Becoming Chinese American: A History of Communities and Institutions* by Him Mark Lai
>
> *The Ethnic Canon: Histories, Institutions, and Interventions* and *Asian/American: Historical Crossings of a Racial Frontier* by David Palumbo-Liu
>
> *Strangers from a Different Shore: A History of Asian Americans* by Ronald Takaki
>
> *The Asian American Movement* by William Wei
>
> *Asian American Studies: A Reader* edited by Jean Yu-Wen Shen Wu and Min Song
>
> *Contemporary Asian America: A Multidisciplinary Reader* edited by Min Zhou and James V. Gatewood

Given the popularity of her works among general readers as well as the critical attention they have received from scholars, Tan holds an important position in Asian American literature and literary studies. Readers who wish to further explore this field can read

> *Crossing Oceans: Reconfiguring American Literary Studies in the Pacific Rim* edited by Noelle Brada-Williams and Karen Chow
>
> *Politicizing Asian American Literature: Towards a Critical Multiculturalism* by Youngsuk Chae
>
> *Asian American Literature: An Annotated Bibliography* by King-Kok Cheung and Stan Yogi
>
> *Imagine Otherwise: On Asian Americanist Critique* by Kandice Chuh

Literary Gestures: The Aesthetic in Asian American Writing edited by Rocío G. Davis and Sue-Im Lee

Asian American Literature in the International Context: Readings on Fiction, Poetry, and Performance edited by Rocío G. Davis and Sämi Ludwig

The Asian Pacific American Heritage: A Companion to Literature and Arts edited by George J. Leonard

Imagining the Nation: Asian American Literature and Cultural Consent by David Leiwei Li

Reading the Literatures of Asian America edited by Shirley Geok-lin Lim and Amy Ling

Transnational Asian American Literature: Sites and Transits edited by Shirley Geok-lin Lim, John Blair Gamber, Stephen Hong Sohn, and Gina Valentino

Immigrant Subjectivities in Asian American and Asian Diapora Literatures and *The Deathly Embrace: Orientalism and Asian American Identity* by Sheng-mei Ma

Asian American Literature: Reviews and Criticism of Works by American Writers of Asian Descent by Lawrence Trudeau

Asian North American Identities: Beyond the Hyphen edited by Eleanor Ty and Donald C. Goellnicht

The Politics of the Visible in Asian North American Narratives by Eleanor Ty

Reading Asian American Literature: From Necessity to Extravagance by Sau-ling Cynthia Wong

In her compelling stories, Tan successfully intertwines various elements and examines issues of identity, immigrant experience, family, and love. The complexity and multiplicity of her novels thus have added a new dimension to contemporary American fiction. Books regarding Asian diaspora and immigration to the United States that might be of interest to readers include

Psycho-Social Adaptation and the Meaning of Achievement for Chinese Immigrants by Lee-Beng Chua

Under Western Eyes: Personal Essays from Asian America edited by Garrett Hongo

Across the Pacific: Asian Americans and Globalization edited by Evelyn Hu-DeHart

Asian Americans: Comparative and Global Perspectives edited by Shirley Hune, Hyung-chan Kim, Stephen S. Fugita, and Amy Ling

Chinese Americans and Their Immigrant Parents: Conflict, Identity, and Values by May Paomay Tung

Chinese American Voices: From the Gold Rush to the Present edited by Judy Yung, Gordon H. Chang, and Him Mark Lai

As one of the most successful ethnic writers in contemporary America, Tan's name appears frequently in multicultural discussion, curricula development, and other related areas. Readers who enjoy the themes of ethnicity and identity reflected in her books might want to read other works related to ethnic American literature:

Borderlands/"La Frontera": The New Mestiza by Gloria Anzaldúa

Cultural Haunting: Ghosts and Ethnicity in Recent American Literature by Kathleen Brogan

American Ethnic Literatures: Native American, African American, Chicano/Latino, and Asian American Writers and Their Backgrounds: An Annotated Bibliography by David R. Peck

The Non-Literate Other: Readings of Illiteracy in Twentieth-Century Novels in English by Helga Ramsey-Kurz

Redefining American Literary History by A. LaVonne Ruoff and Jerry W. Ward Jr.

Besides the vivid characters and engaging stories, Tan's novels are praised for their cultural and historical representations. In *The Joy Luck Club* and *The Kitchen God's Wife*, for example, the characters' personal narratives are closely tied to the historical and cultural contexts of China and Chinese America. Other literary works utilizing a similar narrative strategy include

Winesburg, Ohio by Sherwood Anderson

In Our Time by Ernest Hemingway

The Unvanquished by William Faulkner

The National Endowment for the Arts chose *The Joy Luck Club* for its Big Read program, an initiative to encourage reading and to revitalize the role of literature in American popular culture. Other books in the Big Read program include

Bless Me, Ultima by Rudolfo Anaya

Fahrenheit 451 by Ray Bradbury

My Antonia by Willa Cather

The Great Gatsby by F. Scott Fitzgerald

A Lesson before Dying by Ernest Gaines

The Maltese Falcon by Dashiell Hammett

A Farewell to Arms by Ernest Hemingway

Sun, Stone, and Shadows by Jorge Hernandez
Their Eyes Were Watching God by Zora Neale Hurston
A Wizard of Earthsea by Ursula K. Le Guin
To Kill a Mockingbird by Harper Lee
The Call of the Wild by Jack London
The Thief and the Dogs by Naguib Mahfouz
The Heart Is a Lonely Hunter by Carson McCullers
The Shawl by Cynthia Ozick
Housekeeping by Marilynne Robinson
The Grapes of Wrath by John Steinbeck
The Death of Ivan Ilyich by Leo Tolstoy
The Adventures of Tom Sawyer by Mark Twain
The Age of Innocence by Edith Wharton
Old School by Tobias Wolff

The film adaptation of *The Joy Luck Club* was very well received. Those who are interested in the film may also like other films directed by Wayne Wang and other Asian American-related films (with their directors):

In No One's Shadow: Filipinos in America (Naomi De Castro)
Mississippi Triangle (Christine Choy, Worth Long, Allan Siegel)
Who Killed Vincent Chin? (Christine Choy and Renee Tajima)
The Fall of the I-Hotel (Curtis Choy)
Year of the Dragon (Michael Cimino)
The Color of Honor: The Japanese American Soldier in World War II (Loni Ding)
Forbidden City (PBS: The American Experience, Arthur Dong)
Slaying the Dragon (Deborah Gee)
Picture Bride (Kayo Hatta)
1000 Pieces of Gold (Nancy Kelly)
Pushing Hands (co-directed with Emily Liu), *Eat Drink Man Woman*, *The Wedding Banquet* (Ang Lee)
Fire, Earth, and *Water* (Deepa Mehta)
Surname Viet Given Name Nam (Trinh T. Minh-ha)
Mississippi Masala and *Monsoon Wedding* (Mira Nair)
Monterey's Boat People (Spencer Nakasako and Vincent DiGirolamo)
The World of Suzie Wong (Richard Quine)
A Great Wall (Peter Wang)
Dim Sum: A Little Bit of Heart, Eat a Bowl of Tea, Chan Is Missing, Smoke, and *Chinese Box* (Wayne Wang)
Farewell to Freedom (a production of WCCO-TV)

RESOURCES

Works by Amy Tan (in chronological order)

The Joy Luck Club. New York: G. P. Putnam's Sons, 1989.

"The Language of Discretion." In *State of the Language*, edited by Christopher Ricks and Leonard Michaels, 25–32. Berkeley: University of California Press, 1990.

"Mother Tongue." *Threepenny Review* 43 (Fall 1990): 7–8.

"Two Kinds." In *The Graywolf Annual Seven: Stories from the American Mosaic*, edited by Scott Walker, 188–201. Saint Paul, MN: Graywolf Press, 1990. Reprinted in *The Woman That I Am: The Literature and Culture of Contemporary Women of Color*, edited by D. Soyini Madison, 276–84. New York: St. Martin's Press, 1994.

The Kitchen God's Wife. New York: G. P. Putnam's Sons, 1991.

The Kitchen God's Wife. Audiobook read by Amy Tan. Dove Audio, 1991.

The Moon Lady, illustrated by Gretchen Schields. New York and Toronto: Maxwell MacMillan, 1992.

"Alien Relative." In *Charlie Chan Is Dead: An Anthology of Contemporary Asian American Fiction*, edited by Jessica Hagedorn, 450–61. New York: Penguin, 1993.

"Amy Tan." In *Writers Dreaming*, edited by Naomi Epel, 281–88. New York: Vintage Books, 1994.

The Chinese Siamese Cat, illustrated by Gretchen Schields. New York and Toronto: Maxwell MacMillan, 1994.

The Hundred Secret Senses. New York: G. P. Putnam's Sons, 1995.

The Hundred Secret Senses. Audiobook read by Amy Tan. Dove Audio, 1995.

"Young Girl's Wish." *New Yorker*, October 2, 1995, 80–89.

"Rules of the Game." In *Growing up Ethnic in America: Contemporary Fiction about Learning to be American*, edited by Maria Mazziotti Gillan and Jennifer Gillan, 18–31. New York: Penguin Books, 1999. Reprinted in *Big City Cool: Short Stories about Urban Youth*, edited by M. Jerry Weiss and Helen S. Weiss, 38–50. New York: Viking, 2002.

The Best American Short Stories 1999: Selected from U.S. and Canadian Magazines, co-editor with Katrina Kenison. Boston: Houghton Mifflin Company, 1999.

The Bonesetter's Daughter. New York: G. P. Putnam's Sons, 2001.

"Writers on Writing: Family Ghosts Hoard Secrets That Bewitch the Living." *New York Times*, February 26, 2001. http://www.nytimes.com/2001/02/26/arts/26TAN.html?ex=1215316800&en=5bf0a514348eb63e&ei=5070 (accessed July 7, 2008). Reprinted in *Writers on Writing: More Collected Essays from* The New York Times, Volume II, edited by Jane Smiley, 237–50. New York: Times Books, Henry Holt and Company, 2003.

The Opposite of Fate: A Book of Musings. New York: G. P. Putnam's Sons, 2003.

The Opposite of Fate. Audiobook read by Amy Tan. Brilliance Audio, 2003.

Saving Fish from Drowning. New York: G. P. Putnam's Sons, 2005.

OTHER RESOURCES

Adams, Bella. *Amy Tan.* Manchester and New York: Manchester University Press, 2005.

———. "Identity-in-Difference: Re-Generating Debate about Intergenerational Relationships in Amy Tan's *The Joy Luck Club*." *Studies in the Literary Imagination* 39, no. 2 (2006): 79–94.

———. "*The Joy Luck Club*." The Literary Encyclopedia. June 30, 2002. http://www.litencyc.com/php/sworks.php?rec=true&UID=464 (accessed July 6, 2008).

———. "*The Kitchen God's Wife*." The Literary Encyclopedia. November 8, 2002. http://www.litencyc.com/php/sworks.php?rec=true&UID=440 (accessed July 21, 2008).

———. "Representing History in Amy Tan's *The Kitchen God's Wife*." *MELUS* 28, no. 2 (2003): 9–30.

Allardice, Lisa. "All about Her Mother." *The Guardian.* http://www.guardian.co.uk/books/2005/dec/05/fiction.features11 (accessed March 27, 2009).

"Amy Tan." *Contemporary Authors Online.* Gale Literary Databases. Retrieved July 7, 2008.

"Amy Tan." *Contemporary Literary Criticism.* Gale Literary Databases. Retrieved July 7, 2008.

"Amy Tan." Red Room Writer Profile. http://www.redroom.com/author/amy-tan (accessed July 5, 2008).

"Amy Tan." Special issue, *Hitting Critical Mass: A Journal of Asian American Cultural Criticism* 4, no. 1 (1996).

"Amy Tan: Best-Selling Author of *The Joy Luck Club*." Steven Barclay Agency. http://www.barclayagency.com/tan.html (accessed July 17, 2008).

"Amy Tan: Overview." Brooklyn College. http://academic.brooklyn.cuny.edu/english/melani/cs6/tan.html (accessed July 6, 2008).

"Amy Tan: VG Artist Biography." Voices from the Gaps. http://voices.cla.umn.edu/vg/Bios/entries/tan_amy.html (accessed July 5, 2008).

"Amy Tan Biography: A Uniquely Personal Storyteller." Academy of Achievement. http://www.achievement.org/autodoc/page/tan0bio-1 (accessed July 5, 2008).

"Amy Tan Homepage." Amy Tan. http://amytan.net (accessed July 5, 2008).

"Amy Tan's *The Joy Luck Club*: A Study Guide." *Novels for Students*, vol. 1, chap. 10. Gale Virtual Reference Library. Gale Group, 2002.

"Amy Tan's *The Kitchen God's Wife*: A Study Guide." *Novels for Students*, vol. 13, chap. 15. Gale Virtual Reference Library. Gale Group, 2002.

"Amy Tan's 'Two Kinds': A Study Guide." *Short Stories for Students*, vol. 9, chap. 13. Gale Virtual Reference Library. Gale Group, 2002.

Angier, Carole. "*The Joy Luck Club*." *New Statesman and Society*, June 30, 1989, 35.

"Anniina's Amy Tan Page." http://www.luminarium.org/contemporary/amytan (accessed July 5, 2008).

"Author Profile: Amy Tan." Bookreporter.com. http://www.bookreporter.com/authors/au-tan-amy.asp (accessed July 5, 2008).

Baker, John F. and Calvin Reid. "Fresh Voices, New Audiences." *Publishers Weekly*, August 9, 1993, 32.

Beard, Carla J. *Amy Tan's* The Joy Luck Club, illustrated by Ann Tango-Schurmann. Piscataway, NJ: Research and Education Association, 1996.

Beason, Tyrone. "Tan's Musings Blend Dark and Light, Past and Present." *Seattle Times*, October 31, 2003. http://seattletimes.nwsource.com/cgi-bin/PrintStory.pl?document_id=2001778940&zsection_id=268448483&slug=tan31&date=20031031 (accessed July 21, 2008).

Benjamin, Susan J. "*The Joy Luck Club*." *English Journal* 79, no. 6 (October 1990): 82.

Bennani, Ben, ed. "The World of Amy Tan." Special issue, *Paintbrush: A Journal of Poetry and Translation* 22 (1995).

Bloom, Harold, ed. *Amy Tan*. Philadelphia, PA: Chelsea House Publishers, 2000.

———. *Amy Tan's* The Joy Luck Club. Philadelphia, PA: Chelsea House Publishers, 2003.

Boldt, Chris. "Why Is the Moon Lady in Amy Tan's *The Joy Luck Club* Revealed to Be a Man?" *Notes on Contemporary Literature* 24, no. 4 (1994): 9–10.

Book, Esther Wachs. "*Joy Luck Club* Plays in China: Theatrical Version to be Staged in Five Cities." *Far Eastern Economic Review,* August 26, 1993, 31.

Bow, Leslie. "Cultural Conflict/Feminist Resolution in Amy Tan's *The Joy Luck Club.*" In *New Visions in Asian American Studies: Diversity, Community, Power,* 235–47. Pullman: Washington State University Press, 1994.

BWW News Desk. "*The Joy Luck Club* Extends Off-Broadway through December 1." BroadwayWorld. http://www.broadwayworld.com/printcolumn.cfm?id=22955 (accessed July 8, 2008).

Caesar, Judith. "Patriarchy, Imperialism, and Knowledge in *The Kitchen God's Wife.*" *North Dakota Quarterly* 62, no. 4 (1994–1995): 164–74.

Carr, Jo. "The Hundred Secret Senses." *Library Journal,* May 15, 1996, 100.

Champion, Laurie. "Amy Tan." In *Dictionary of Literary Biography, Volume 312: Asian American Writers,* edited by Deborah L. Madsen, 288–98. Detroit, MI: Thomson Gale, 2005.

Chen, Victoria. "Chinese American Women, Language, and Moving Subjectivity." *Women and Language* 18, no. 1 (1995): 3–7.

Cheng, Scarlet. "Amy Tan Redux." *Belles Lettres* 7, no. 1 (Fall 1991): 15, 19.

———. "Your Mother is in Your Bones." *Belles Lettres* 4, no. 4 (Summer 1989): 12.

Chin, Frank. "Come All Ye Asian American Writers of the Real and the Fake." In *The Big Aiiieeeee! An Anthology of Chinese American and Japanese American Literature,* edited by Jeffery Paul Chan, Frank Chin, Lawson Fusao Inada, and Shawn Wong, 1–91. New York: Meridian, 1991.

Chow, Rey. "Women in the Holocene: Ethnicity, Fantasy, and the Film *The Joy Luck Club*" In *Feminism and the Pedagogies of Everyday Life,* edited by Carmen Luke, 204–21. Albany: State University of New York Press, 1995.

Colker, David. "Learn a Little of Her Story." *Los Angeles Times,* December 22, 1995, E3.

Conceison, Claire A. "Translating Collaboration: *The Joy Luck Club* and Intercultural Theatre." *Drama Review: A Journal of Performance Studies* 39, no. 3 (1995): 151–66.

Connema, Richard. "Two Reviews: O'Neill's *Long Day's Journey into Night* is Superb, *The Joy Luck Club* Has Great Acting in an Uneven Play." Talkin' Broadway. http://www.talkinbroadway.com/regional/sanfran/s20.html (accessed July 10, 2008).

Cooperman, Jeannette Batz. *The Broom Closet: Secret Meanings of Domesticity in Postfeminist Novels by Louise Erdrich, Mary Gordon, Toni*

Morrison, Marge Piercy, Jane Smiley, and Amy Tan. New York: Peter Lang, 1999.

Crow, Kim. "'The Opposite of Fate: A Book of Musings' by Amy Tan." *Pittsburgh Post-Gazette,* December 14, 2003. http://www.post-gazette.com/books/reviews/20031214amytan1214fnp6.asp (accessed July 21, 2008).

Darraj, Susan Muaddi. *Amy Tan.* New York: Chelsea House, 2007.

Davis, Emory. "An Interview with Amy Tan: Fiction 'The Beast that Roars.'" *Writing on the Edge* 1, no. 2 (1990): 97–111.

Davis, Rocío G. "Amy Tan's *The Kitchen God's Wife*: An American Dream Come True—in China." *Notes on Contemporary Literature* 24, no. 5 (1994): 3–5.

———. "Identity in Community in Ethnic Short Story Cycles: Amy Tan's *The Joy Luck Club*, Louise Erdrich's *Love Medicine*, Gloria Naylor's *The Women of Brewster Place*." In *Ethnicity and the American Short Story,* edited by Julie Brown, 3–23. New York: Garland, 1997.

de Bertodano, Helena. "A Life Stranger than Fiction." Telegraph.co.uk, Nov. 10, 2003. http://www.telegraph.co.uk/arts/main.jhtml?xml=/arts/2003/11/11/boamy10.xml/ (accessed March 27, 2009).

Delucchi, Michael. "Self and Identity among Aging Immigrants in *The Joy Luck Club*." *Journal of Aging and Identity* 3, no. 2 (1998): 59–66.

Denison, D. C. "Amy Tan." *Boston Sunday Globe*, June 28, 1991, 8.

Dew, Robb Forman. "Pangs of an Abandoned Child." *New York Times,* June 16, 1991, 9. http://www.nytimes.com/books/01/02/18/specials/tan-kitchen.html/ (accessed March 27, 2009).

DiYanni, Robert. *Literature: Approaches to Fiction, Poetry, and Drama.* 2nd ed. New York: McGraw-Hill, 2008.

Dong, Lan. a. "Amy Tan." In *Encyclopedia of Multiethnic American Literature,* edited by Emmanuel S. Nelson, 2131–36. Westport, CT: Greenwood, 2005.

———. b. "*The Joy Luck Club*." In *Encyclopedia of Multiethnic American Literature,* edited by Emmanuel S. Nelson, 1205–06. Westport, CT: Greenwood, 2005.

———. c. "Maxine Hong Kingston." In *Encyclopedia of Multiethnic American Literature,* edited by Emmanuel S. Nelson, 1251–53. Westport, CT: Greenwood, 2005.

Donovan, Mary Ann. "*The Joy Luck Club*." *America,* November 17, 1990, 372.

Dooley, Susan. "Mah-Jong and the Ladies of the Club." *Washington Post Book World,* March 5, 1989, 7.

Dorris, Michael. "Mothers and Daughters." *Chicago Tribune Books,* March 12, 1989, 1, 11.

Doten, Patti. "Sharing Her Mother's Secrets." *Boston Globe,* June 21, 1991, 63.

Duke, Michael. "Red Ivy, and Green Earth Mother." *World Literature Today* 65, no. 2 (Spring 1991): 361.

Dunick, Lisa M. S. "The Silencing Effect of Canonicity: Authorship and the Written Word in Amy Tan's Novels." *MELUS* 31, no. 2 (2006): 3–20.

Ellefson, Elias. "Amy Tan." In *A Reader's Companion to the Short Story in English,* edited by Erin Fallon, 398–403. Westport, CT: Greenwood, 2001.

Emerick, Ronald. "The Role of Mah Jong in Amy Tan's *The Joy Luck Club.*" *CEA Critic: An Official Journal of the College English Association* 61, no. 2–3 (1999): 37–45.

Feldman, Gayle. "*The Joy Luck Club*: Chinese Magic, American Blessings, and a Publishing Fairy Tale." *Publishers Weekly,* July 7, 1989, 24.

Feng, Pin-chia. "Amy Tan." In *Dictionary of Literary Biography, Volume 173: American Novelists since World War II,* edited by James R. Giles and Wanda H. Giles, 281–89. Detroit, MI: Gale, 1996.

Fisher, Ann H. "*The Joy Luck Club.*" *Library Journal,* February 15, 1989, 178.

Fitzgerald, Penelope. "Luck Dispensers." *London Review of Books*, July 11, 1991, 19.

Fong, Rowena. "*The Joy Luck Club.*" *The Gerontologist* 35, no. 2 (April 1995): 284.

Fortuna, Diane. "*The Hundred Secret Senses.*" *America,* May 4, 1996, 27.

Gately, Patricia. "Ten Thousand Different Ways: Inventing Mothers, Inventing Hope." *Paintbrush: A Journal of Poetry and Translation* 22 (1995): 51–55.

Gates, David. "*The Joy Luck Club.*" *Newsweek,* April 17, 1989, 68–69.

Gee, Lisa. "*Saving Fish from Drowning*, by Amy Tan." *The Independent,* November 18, 2005. http://www.independent.co.uk/arts-entertainment/books/reviews/saving-fish-from-drowning-by-amy-tan-515716.html (accessed July 22, 2008).

Giles, Gretchen. "Ghost Writer: Bay Area Author Amy Tan Talks about Fame and Phantoms." *The Sonoma Independent,* December 14–20, 1995. http://www.metroactive.com/papers/sonoma/12.14.95/tan-9550.html (accessed July 7, 2008).

Gillespie, Elgy. "Amy Angst, and the Second Novel." *San Francisco Review of Books* 16, no. 1 (Summer 1991): 33–34.

Green, Suzanne D. "Thematic Deviance or Poetic License? The Filming of *The Joy Luck Club.*" In *Vision/Revision: Adapting Contemporary American Fiction by Women to Film*, edited by Barbara Tepa Lupack, 211–25. Bowling Green, OH: Popular, 1996.

Greenlaw, Lavinia. "The Owl's Story." *Time Literary Supplement,* February 16, 1996, 22.

Hamilton, Patricia L. "Feng Shui, Astrology, and the Five Elements: Traditional Chinese Belief in Amy Tan's *The Joy Luck Club.*" *MELUS* 24, no. 2 (1999): 125–45.

Hayn, Judith and Deborah Sherrill. "Female Protagonists in Multicultural Young Adult Literature: Sources and Strategies." *Alan Review* 24, no. 1 (1996). http://scholar.lib.vt.edu/ejournals/ALAN/fall96/f96-09-Hayn.html (accessed November 11, 2008).

Henderson, Katherine Usher. "Amy Tan." In *Inter/View: Talks with America's Writing Women,* by Mickey Pearlman and Katherine Usher Henderson, 15–22. Lexington: University Press of Kentucky, 1990.

Ho, Khanh. "*The Kitchen God's Wife.*" *Amerasia Journal* 19, no. 2 (Spring 1993): 181.

Ho, Wendy Ann. *In Her Mother's House: The Politics of Asian American Mother-Daughter Writing.* Walnut Creek, CA: AltaMira Press, 1999.

———. "Swan-Feather Mothers and Coca-Cola Daughters: Teaching Amy Tan's *The Joy Luck Club.*" In *Teaching American Ethnic Literatures: Nineteen Essays,* edited by John R. Maitino and David R. Peck, 327–45. Albuquerque: University of New Mexico Press, 1996.

Hoffman, Marion B. *The Joy Luck Club: A Unit Plan.* Berlin, MD: Teacher's Pet Publications, 1999.

Hoffman, Preston. "Book Sounds." *Wilson Library Bulletin* 69, no. 7 (March 1995): 99.

Hoggard, Liz. "Death as a Source of Life." *The Observer,* November 23, 2003. http://www.guardian.co.uk/books/2003/nov/23/fiction.features1 (accessed July 22, 2008).

Hoyte, Kirsten Dinnall. "Contradiction and Culture: Revisiting Amy Tan's 'Two Kinds' (Again)." *Minnesota Review* 61–62 (2004): 161–69.

Hubbard, Kim and Maria Wilhelm. "*The Joy Luck Club* Has Brought Writer Amy Tan a Bit of Both." *People Weekly,* April 10, 1989, 149–50.

Hum, Sue. "Articulating Authentic Chineseness: The Politics of Reading Race and Ethnicity Aesthetically." In *Relations, Locations, Positions: Composition Theory for Writing Teachers*, edited by Peter Vandenberg, Sue Hum, and Jennifer Clary-Lemon, 442–70. Urbana, IL: National Council of Teachers of English, 2006.

Huntley, E. D. *Amy Tan: A Critical Companion.* Westport, CT: Greenwood, 1998.

"Interview with Amy Tan." BBC Online. http://www.bbc.co.uk/religion/programmes/belief/scripts/amy_tan.shtml (accessed July 8, 2008).

Ives, Nancy R. "*The Hundred Secret Senses.*" *Library Journal,* January 1996, 166.

Iyer, Pico. "The Second Triumph of Amy Tan." *Time,* June 3, 1991. http://www.time.com/time/printout/0,8816,973101,00.html (accessed July 21, 2008).

"*The Joy Luck Club.*" CliffsNotes. http://www.cliffsnotes.com/WileyCDA/LitNote/The-Joy-Luck-Club.id-39.html (accessed July 6, 2008).

"*The Joy Luck Club.*" IPL Online Literary Criticism Collection. http://www.ipl.org/div/litcrit/bin/litcrit.out.pl?ti=joy-272 (accessed July 6, 2008).

"*The Joy Luck Club.*" Penguin Group (USA). http://us.penguingroup.com/nf/Book/BookDisplay/0,,9780143038092,00.html (accessed July 6, 2008).

"*The Joy Luck Club.*" SparkNotes. http://www.sparknotes.com/lit/joyluck (accessed July 6, 2008).

"*The Joy Luck Club.*" Teach With Movies. http://www.teachwithmovies.org/guides/joy-luck-club.html (accessed July 6, 2008).

"*The Joy Luck Club.*" 2008 SFIAAFF Film Guide. http://filmguide.festival.asianamericanmedia.org/tixSYS/2008/filmguide/eventnote.php?EventNumber=1063&notepg=1 (accessed July 6, 2008).

"*The Joy Luck Club* Book Notes Summary." BookRags. http://www.bookrags.com/notes/jlc/ (accessed July 6, 2008).

"*The Joy Luck Club* Extends by One Week." *New York Theatre Guide,* November 13, 2007. http://www.newyorktheatreguide.com/news/nov07/joy13nov07.htm (accessed July 8, 2008).

"*The Joy Luck Club* Movie Reviews." IGN Entertainment. http://www.rottentomatoes.com/m/joy_luck_club/ (accessed July 6, 2008).

"*The Joy Luck Club* (Off-Broadway)." Broadway.com. http://www.broadway.com/gen/show.aspx?SI=553361 (accessed July 8, 2008).

"*The Joy Luck Club* Summary and Study Guide." eNotes. http://www.enotes.com/joy-luck (accessed July 6, 2008).

Kafka, Phillipa. "Amy Tan, *The Kitchen God's Wife*: 'Chasing Away a Big Stink.'" In *(Un)Doing the Missionary Position: Gender Symmetry in Contemporary Asian American Women's Writing,* 17–50. Westport, CT: Greenwood Press, 1997.

———. "Erecting a Statue of an Unknown Goddess in Amy Tan's *The Kitchen God's Wife* (1991)." In *Women Making Art: Women in the Visual, Literary, and Performing Arts since 1960,* edited by Deborah Johnson and Wendy Oliver, 189–210. New York: Peter Lang, 2001.

Kakutani, Michiko. "Sisters Looking for Ghosts in China." *New York Times,* November 17, 1995, B13.

Kelsey, Rioux. "*The Hundred Secret Senses.*" *Teen Ink,* February 2007, 49.

Kepner, Susan. "Imagine This: The Amazing Adventure of Amy Tan." *San Francisco Examiner Focus,* May 1989, 58–60, 161–62.

Kim, Elaine H. "'Such Opposite Creatures': Men and Women in Asian American Literature." *Michigan Quarterly Review* 29 (1990): 68–92.

"*The Kitchen God's Wife*." 500 Great Books by Women. http://www.tuvy. com/resource/books/k/Kitchen_Gods_Wife.html (accessed July 6, 2008).

"*The Kitchen God's Wife*." Answers.com. http://www.answers.com/topic/ the-kitchen-god-s-wife (accessed July 6, 2008).

"*The Kitchen God's Wife*." SparkNotes. http://www.sparknotes.com/lit/ kitchengods/ (accessed July 6, 2008).

"*The Kitchen God's Wife* Summary and Analysis." BookRags. http://www. bookrags.com/The_Kitchen_God's_Wife (accessed July 6, 2008).

"*The Kitchen God's Wife* Summary and Study Guide." eNotes. http://www. enotes.com/kitchen-gods (accessed July 6, 2008).

Koenig, Marlene. "With a Little Bit of Joy and Luck." *Eureka Studies in Teaching Short Fiction* 1, no. 2 (2001): 11–14.

Kort, Carol. "Tan, Amy Ruth." In *A to Z of American Women Writers*, 211–13. New York: Facts on File, 2000.

Kramer, Babara. *Amy Tan, Author of* The Joy Luck Club. Springfield, NJ: Enslow Publishers, 1996.

Lee, Ken-fang. "Cultural Translation and the Exorcist: A Reading of Kingston's and Tan's Ghost Stories." *MELUS* 29, no. 2 (2004): 105–27.

Lew, Julie. "How Stories Written for Mother Became Amy Tan's Bestseller." *New York Times,* July 4, 1989, 23.

Lipson, Eden Ross. "The Wicked English-Speaking Daughter." *New York Times Book Review,* March 19, 1989, 3.

Longenecker, Donna. "Relationship with Mother Helped Tan Hone Writing Skills." *UB Reporter,* March 27, 2003. http://www.buffalo.edu/ubreporter/ archives/vol34/vol34n18/articles/AmyTan.html (accessed July 23, 2008).

López Morell, Beatriz. "Chinese Women's Celebration in America in *The Joy Luck Club*." In *Evolving Origins, Transplanting Cultures: Literary Legacies of the New Americans,* edited by Laura P. Alonso Gallo and Antonia Dominguez Miguela, 77–85. Spain: Universidad de Huelva, 2002.

Lux, Elaine. "Narrative Bones: Amy Tan's *Bonesetter's Daughter* and Hugh Cook's *Homecoming Man*." In *The Gift of Story: Narrating Hope in a Postmodern World,* edited by Emily Griesinger and Mark A. Easton, 117–32. Waco, TX: Baylor University Press, 2006.

Lyall, Sarah. "In the Country of the Spirits: At Home with Writer Amy Tan." *New York Times,* December 28, 1995, B1.

———. "A Writer Knows that Spirits Dwell Beyond Her Pages." *New York Times,* December 29, 1995, B1.

Ma, Sheng-mei. "Amy Tan's *The Chinese Siamese Cat*: Chinoiserie and Ethnic Stereotypes." *The Lion and the Unicorn: A Critical Journal of Children's Literature* 23, no. 2 (1999): 202–18.

———. "'Chinese and Dogs' in Amy Tan's *The Hundred Secret Senses*: Ethnicizing the Primitive a la New Age." *MELUS* 26, no. 1 (2001): 29–44.

———. *The Deathly Embrace: Orientalism and Asian American Identity.* Minneapolis: University of Minnesota Press, 2000.

MacDonald, Jay. "A Date with Fate: Tan's Memoir Probes Cosmic Connections." BookPage. November 2003. http://www.bookpage.com/0311bp/amy_tan.html (accessed July 23, 2008).

Mandell, Jonathan. "Her Mother, Her Muse." *Newsday,* July 15, 1991, 42.

Marvis, Barbara J. *Contemporary American Success Stories: Famous People of Asian Ancestry.* Childs, MD: Mitchell Lane Publishers, 1995.

Maslin, Janet. "*The Joy Luck Club.*" *New York Times,* September 8, 1993, C15.

Mason, Deborah. "A Not-So-Dutiful Daughter." *New York Times,* November 23, 2003. http://query.nytimes.com/gst/fullpage.html?res=9A05E6DD1438 F930A15752C1A9659C8B63 (accessed July 22, 2008).

Maxey, Ruth. "The 'East is Where Things Begin': Writing the Ancestral Homeland in Amy Tan and Maxine Hong Kingston." *Orbis Litterarum* 60, no. 1 (2005): 1–15.

McAlister, Melanie. "(Mis)Reading *The Joy Luck Club.*" *Asian American: Journal of Culture and the Arts* 1 (Winter 1992): 102–18.

McCarthy, Todd. "*The Joy Luck Club.*" *Variety,* September 13, 1993, 32.

McGinnis, John. "*The Joy Luck Club.*" *Wall Street Journal,* August 19, 1993, A8.

Memmott, Carol. "Tan's 'Fish' Will Hook Readers." *USA Today,* October 31, 2005. http://www.usatoday.com/life/books/reviews/2005-10-31-amy-tan_x.htm (accessed July 22, 2008).

Merina, Anita. "Joy, Luck, and Literature." *NEA Today* 10, no. 3 (October 1991): 9.

Mesic, Penelope. "Sisterly Bonds." *Chicago Tribue Books,* November 5, 1995, 1, 11.

Messud, Claire. "Ghost Story." *New York Times Book Review* (October 29, 1995): 11.

———. "What's Safe to Say." Telegraph. November 19, 2003. http://www.telegraph.co.uk/culture/books/3606692/what's-safe-to-say.html/ (accessed March 27, 2009).

Mielke, Robert. "'American Translation': *The Joy Luck Club* as Film." *Paintbrush: A Journal of Poetry and Translation* 22 (1995): 68–75.

Miner, Valerie. "*The Joy Luck Club.*" *Nation,* April 24, 1989, 566.

Mistri, Zenobia. "Discovering the Ethnic Name and the Genealogical Tie in Amy Tan's *The Joy Luck Club.*" *Studies in Short Fiction* 35, no. 3 (1998): 251–57.

Mones, Nicole. "China Syndrome." *Washington Post Book World,* February 11, 2001, 4.

Morrison, Donald. "Review of *Saving Fish from Drowning*." *Time International,* December 5, 2005, 6.

Nadeau, Frances A. "The Mother/Daughter Relationship in Young Adult Fiction." *Alan Review* 22, no. 2 (1995). http://scholar.lib.vt.edu/ejournals/ALAN/winter95/Nadeau.html (accessed November 11, 2008).

Nathan, Paul. "Tan Teams up for Encore." *Publishers Weekly,* September 5, 1994, 20.

"*New York Times* Featured Author: Amy Tan." New York Times. http://www.nytimes.com/books/01/02/18/specials/tan.html (accessed July 5, 2008).

Nurse, Donna. "A Review of *The Hundred Secret Senses*." *Maclean's,* November 6, 1995, 85.

Olson, Carol Booth and Pat Clark. "Using Amy Tan's 'The Moon Lady' to Teach Analytical Writing in the Multicultural Classroom." *Paintbrush: A Journal of Poetry and Translation* 22 (1995): 85–98.

Ong, Caroline. "Re-Writing the Old Wives Tales." *Times Literary Supplement,* July 5, 1991, 20.

———"Roots Relations." *Times Literary Supplement,* December 29, 1989, 1447.

"Online Study Guide for *The Joy Luck Club*." Monkey Notes. http://www.pinkmonkey.com/booknotes/monkeynotes/pmJoyLuckClub01.asp (accessed July 6, 2008).

Paik, Felicia. "*The Hundred Secret Senses*." *Ms. Magazine,* November-December 1995, 88.

Pavey, Ruth. "A Review of *The Hundred Secret Senses*." *New Statesman and Society* 9, no. 390 (February 1996): 38.

Peter, Nelson and Peter Freundlich. "Women We Love: Nine Who Knock Us Out." *Esquire,* August 1989, 86.

Pollard, D. E. "Much Ado About Identity." *Far Eastern Economic Review,* July 27, 1989, 41.

"Reading at Risk: A Survey of Literary Reading in America." National Endowment for the Arts. June 2004. www.nea.gov/pub/ReadingAtRisk.pdf (accessed November 11, 2008).

Reese, Jennifer. "Review of *Saving Fish from Drowning*." *Entertainment Weekly,* October 21, 2005, 78.

Riley, Sheila. "*The Hundred Secret Senses*." *Library Journal,* November 15, 1995, 101.

Roback, Diane and Shannon Maughan. "Fall 1992 Childrens Books." *Publishers Weekly,* July 20, 1992, 35.

Robinson, Mei Li. *The Kitchen God's Wife: Notes*. Lincoln, NE: John Wiley and Sons, 1996.

Romagnolo, Catherine. "Narrative Beginnings in Amy Tan's *The Joy Luck Club*: A Feminist Study." *Studies in the Novel* 35, no. 1 (2003): 89–107.

Rosinsky, Natalie M. *Amy Tan: Author and Storyteller*. Minneapolis, MN: Compass Point Books, 2007.

Rothstein, Mervyn. "A New Novel by Amy Tan, Who's Still Trying to Adapt to Success." *New York Times,* June 11, 1991, 13C–14C.

Rozakis, Laurie Neu. *The Joy Luck Club: Notes*. Lincoln, NE: John Wiley and Sons, 1994.

Rubin, Merle. "Chinese-American 'Bridge' Club." *Christian Science Monitor,* April 21, 1989, 13.

Sachs, Andrea. "The Joys and Sorrows of Amy Tan." *Time,* February 19, 2001, 72.

"Saving Fish from Drowning." Booklist, February 1, 2006, 76.

"Saving Fish from Drowning." Publishers Weekly, March 6, 2006, 68.

Schecter, Ellen. "The Moon Lady." *New York Times Book Review,* November 8, 1992, 31.

Schell, Orville. "Your Mother is in Your Bones." *New York Times,* March 19, 1989, 3, 28.

Scott, Margaret. "California Chinoiserie." *Far Eastern Economic Review,* May 30, 1996, 37.

Seaman, Donna. "The Booklist Interview: Amy Tan." *Booklist,* October 1, 1990, 256–57.

See, Carolyn. "Drowning in America, Starving for China." *Los Angeles Times Book Review,* March 12, 1989, 1, 11.

Shanley, Roger W. "Novel Choices, Pun Intended." *English Journal* 95, no. 3 (2006): 11–13.

Shapiro, Laura. "The Generation Gap in Chinatown." *Newsweek,* September 27, 1993, 70.

———. "Ghost Story." *Newsweek,* November 6, 1995, 91.

———. "*The Kitchen God's Wife.*" *Newsweek,* June 24, 1991, 63.

Shaw, Jessica. "Review of *The Opposite of Fate: A Book of Musings*." *Entertainment Weekly,* November 7, 2003, 76.

Shea, Renée H. and Deborah L. Wilchek. *Amy Tan in the Classroom: The Art of Invisible Strength*. Urbana, IL: National Council of Teachers of English, 2005.

Shear, Walter. "Generational Differences and the Diaspora in *The Joy Luck Club*." *Critique: Studies in Contemporary Fiction* 34, no. 3 (Spring 1993): 193–99.

Shen, Gloria. "Born of a Stranger: Mother-Daughter Relationships and Storytelling in Amy Tan's *The Joy Luck Club*." In *International Women's Writing: New Landscapes of Identity*, edited by Anne E. Brown and Marjane E. Goozé, 233–44. Westport, CT: Greenwood Press, 1995.

Shilling, Jane. "What the Memory Box Holds." Telegraph.co.uk. November 17, 2003. http://www.telegraph.co.uk/arts/main.jhtml?xml=/arts/2003/11/16/botan216.xml (accessed July 22, 2008).

Simon, Glea. "Amy Tan Explores the Interweaving of Fate, Fact and Fiction: Tan Takes a Look at Her Work, Life." *The San Francisco Chronicle*, December 7, 2003, M1.

Simpson, Janice C. and Pico Iyer. "Fresh Voices Above the Noisy Din: New Works by Four Chinese-American Writers Splendidly Illustrate the Frustrations, Humor, and Eternal Wonder of the Immigrant's Life." *Time*, June 3, 1991, 66.

Skow, John. "Tiger Ladies." *Time*, March 27, 1989, 98.

Smith, Holly. "The Kitchen God's Wife." 500 Great Books by Women. http://www.tuvy.com/resource/books/k/Kitchen_Gods_Wife.html (accessed July 21, 2008).

Smith, Jayne R. *The Joy Luck Club: A Curriculm Unit*. Rocky River, OH: Center for Learning, 1994.

Smith, Wendy. "*The Kitchen God's Wife* by Amy Tan." CheneySmith.com. http://www.cheneysmith.com/wen/kitchen.htm (accessed July 21, 2008).

Snodgrass, Mary Ellen. *Amy Tan: A Literary Companion*. Jefferson, NC: McFarland, 2004.

Solomon, Andrew. "'Saving Fish from Drowning': Bus of Fools." *The New York Times*, October 16, 2005, 22.

Solomon, Julie. "*The Joy Luck Club*." *Wall Street Journal*, September 9, 1993, A18.

Somogyi, Barbara and David Stanton. "Interview with Amy Tan." *Poets and Writers* 19 (September-October 1991): 24–32.

Souris, Stephen. "'Only Two Kinds of Daughters': Inter-Monologue Dialogicity in *The Joy Luck Club*." *MELUS* 19, no. 2 (1994): 99–124.

Spalding, Frances. "*The Joy Luck Club*." *Times Educational Supplement*, August 4, 1989, 19.

Sparrow, Joyce. "Review of *The Opposite of Fate*." *Library Journal*, November 15, 2003, 68.

"The Spirit Within, Salon Interview: Amy Tan." Salon.com. http://www.salon.com/12nov1995/feature/tan.html (accessed July 5, 2008).

Stanton, David. "Breakfast with Amy Tan." *Paintbrush: A Journal of Poetry and Translation* 22 (1995): 5–19.

Steinberg, Sybil and Genevieve Stuttaford. "*The Joy Luck Club*." *Publishers Weekly*, December 23, 1988, 66.

Sterritt, David. "*The Joy Luck Club*." *Christian Science Monitor*, September 16, 1993, 11.

Streitfeld, David. "The 'Luck' of Amy Tan." *Washington Post*, October 8, 1989, F1.

Su, Karen Kai-Yuan. "'Just Translating': The Politics of Translation and Ethnography in Chinese American Women's Writing." PhD diss., University of California at Berkeley, 1998.

Sweeting, Paul and John Zinsser. "*The Joy Luck Club.*" *Publishers Weekly,* July 7, 1989, 37.

"Talk by U.S. Writer Amy Tan Prevented." *Los Angeles Times,* April 1, 1996, A8.

"Tan, Amy." *Current Biography* 53, no. 2 (February 1992): 55.

Tibbetts, John C. "A Delicate Balance: An Interview with Wayne Wang about *The Joy Luck Club.*" *Literature/Film Quarterly* 22, no. 1 (1994): 2–6.

Truzzi, Gianni. "'Joy Luck Club' Mirrors Their Own Generational Conflicts, Actors Say." *Seattle Post-Intelligencer.* January 3, 2003. http://seattlepi. nwsource.com/theater/102559_fanf03.shtml (accessed July 10, 2008).

Tseo, George. "Joy Luck: The Perils of Transcultural 'Translation.'" *Literature/Film Quarterly* 24, no. 4 (1996): 338–43.

Tyler, Patrick. "*The Joy Luck Club.*" *New York Times,* November 27, 1993, N9.

Tynan, Laurie. "*The Joy Luck Club.*" *Library Journal,* July 1989, 123.

Unali, Linda. "Americanization and Hybridization in *The Hundred Secret Senses.*" *Hitting Critical Mass* 4, no. 1 (1996): 135–44.

Venkatasubban, Ragini. "*The Kitchen God's Wife.*" *Teen Ink,* June 2007, 42.

Visaya, Momar G. "FilAm Talents Shine in *The Joy Luck Club.*" The Asian Journal Blog. http://asianjournal.wordpress.com/2007/11/10/filam-talents-shine-in-the-joy-luck-club/ (accessed July 8, 2008).

"Vocabulary from *The Joy Luck Club.*" Vocabulary Classic Texts. http://www. vocabulary.com/VUctjoyluck.html (accessed July 6, 2008).

Wagner, Tamara S. "'After Another Round of Tissues': 'Bad Time' Fiction and the Amy Tan Syndrome in Recent Singaporean Novels." *Journal of Commonwealth Literature* 38, no. 2 (2003): 19–39.

Wang, Dorothy. "*The Joy Luck Club.*" *Newsweek,* April 17, 1989, 69.

Wang, Wayne, director. *The Joy Luck Club.* DVD. Burbank, CA: Buena Vista Home Video, 2002.

Wiener, Gary, ed. *Women's Issues in Amy Tan's* The Joy Luck Club. Detroit, MI: Greenhaven Press, 2008.

Willard, Nancy. "Talking to Ghosts." *New York Times Book Review,* February 18, 2001, 9.

Wong, Sau-ling Cynthia. "'Sugar Sisterhood': Situating the Amy Tan Phenomenon." In *The Ethnic Canon: Histories, Institutions, and Interventions,* edited by David Palumbo-Liu, 174–210. Minneapolis: Minnesota University Press, 1995.

Woo, Elaine. "Striking Cultural Sparks." *Los Angeles Times,* March 12, 1989, Part VI, 1–14.

Woo, Eunjoo. "'The Things I Must Not Forget': Chinese American Mother/ Daughter Conflict and Reconciliation in Amy Tan's *The Bonesetter's Daughter.*" *Feminist Studies in English Literature* 12, no. 1 (2004): 129–49.

Xu, Ben. "Memory and the Ethnic Self: Reading Amy Tan's *The Joy Luck Club*." *MELUS* 19, no. 1 (1994): 3–18.

Xu, Wenying. "Amy Tan." In *Asian American Novelists: A Bio-Bibliographical Critical Sourcebook*, edited by Emmanuel S. Nelson, 365–73. Westport, CT: Greenwood, 2000.

———. "A Womanist Production of Truths: The Use of Myths in Amy Tan." *Paintbrush: A Journal of Poetry and Translation* 22 (1995): 56–66.

Yglesias, Helen. "The Second Time Around: A Review of *The Kitchen God's Wife*." *Women's Review of Books* 8, no. 12 (September 1991): 1, 3.

Yin, J. "Constructing the Other: A Critical Reading of *The Joy Luck Club*." *Howard Journal of Communication* 16 (2005): 149–75.

Young, Pamela. "Mother with a Past: The Family Album Inspires a Gifted Writer." *Maclean's*, July 15, 1991, 47.

Yu, Su-lin. "Sisterhood as Cultural Difference in Amy Tan's *The Hundred Secret Senses* and Cristina García's *The Aguero Sisters*." *Critique: Studies in Contemporary Fiction* 47, no. 4 (2006): 345–61.

Yuan, Yuan. "Mothers' 'China Narrative': Amy Tan's *The Joy Luck Club* and *The Kitchen God's Wife*." In *The Chinese in America: A History from Gold Mountain to the New Millennium*, edited by Susie Lan Cassel, 351–64. Walnut Creek, CA: AltaMira, 2002.

———"The Semiotics of China Narratives in the Con/Texts of Kingston and Tan." *Critique: Studies in Contemporary Fiction* 40, no. 3 (1999): 292–303.

Zeng, Li. "Diasporic Self, Cultural Other: Negotiating Ethnicity through Transformation in the Fiction of Tan and Kingston." *Language and Literature* 28 (2003): 1–15.

Zhang, Benzi. "Reading Amy Tan's Hologram: *The Hundred Secret Senses*." *International Fiction Review* 31, no. 1–2 (2004): 13–18.

INDEX

About the Author

LAN DONG is assistant professor of English at the University of Illinois at Springfield.